Let's Create, Together!

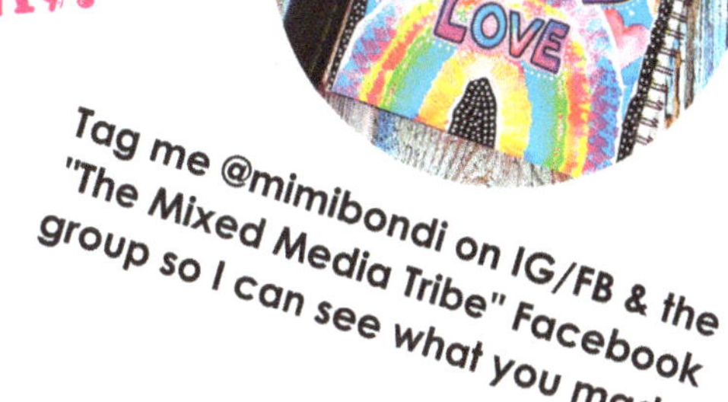

Go On, Tear It Up :-)

Books in The Secret Stash collection are made for collage, and to inspire you to create more art!! Think art journaling, greeting cards, junk journals, art tags & more!

Tag me @mimibondi on IG/FB & the "The Mixed Media Tribe" Facebook group so I can see what you made!

Let's Keep In Touch:

The best way is via my newsletter! Be the first to know about new books, classes, sales and exclusive goodies :)

If You Enjoyed This Book...

Please consider leaving a positive review on Amazon (or my website). There are a few books available in this series and I'd love to create even more of them for you :)

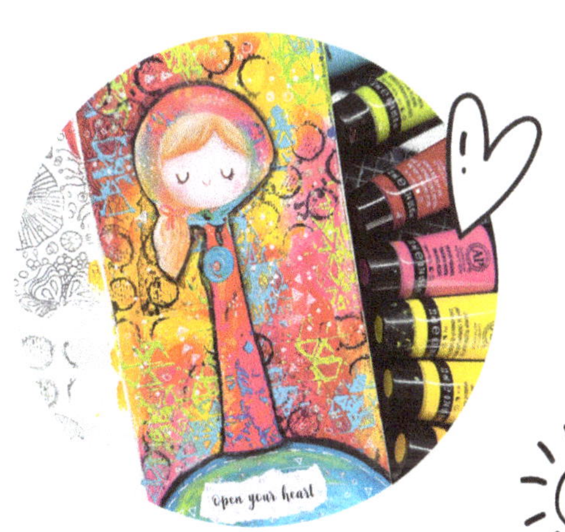

Come Say Hi!

Visit my 'online home' at **MIMIBONDI.COM** for:
* Hundreds of mixed media **printables** to download
* Tons of free mixed media **tutorials**
* Mixed media **classes,** books, prints & more

Now let's make some art!!!

xo Mimi-Bondi

Mixed media artist, illustrator, graphic/web designer, author & peanut M&M's addict!

Thank You For Purchasing This Book, You Rock!

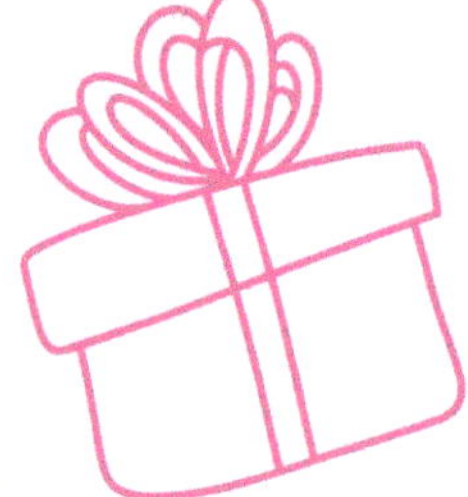

I HAVE A GIFT FOR YOU!

To thank you for purchasing my book, please download a surprise Fluffy Skies printable (not available in this book) - for free!

Simply go to:

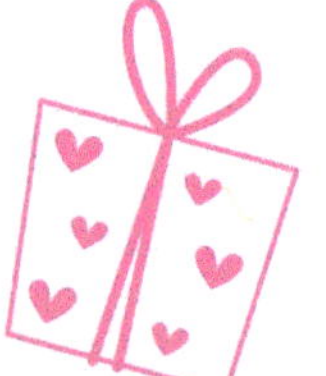

- **mimibondi.com** then **'Secret Stash Store'**
- Type **Fluffy Skies Printable 1** in the search bar
- Enter coupon code **AZFLSFR94F** at checkout

mimibondi.com

Thank you for reading...

Now go and create something awesome!!

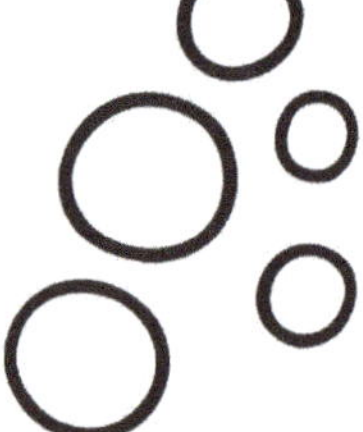
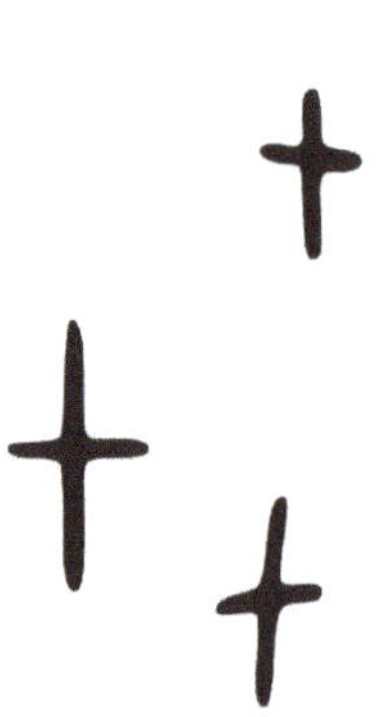

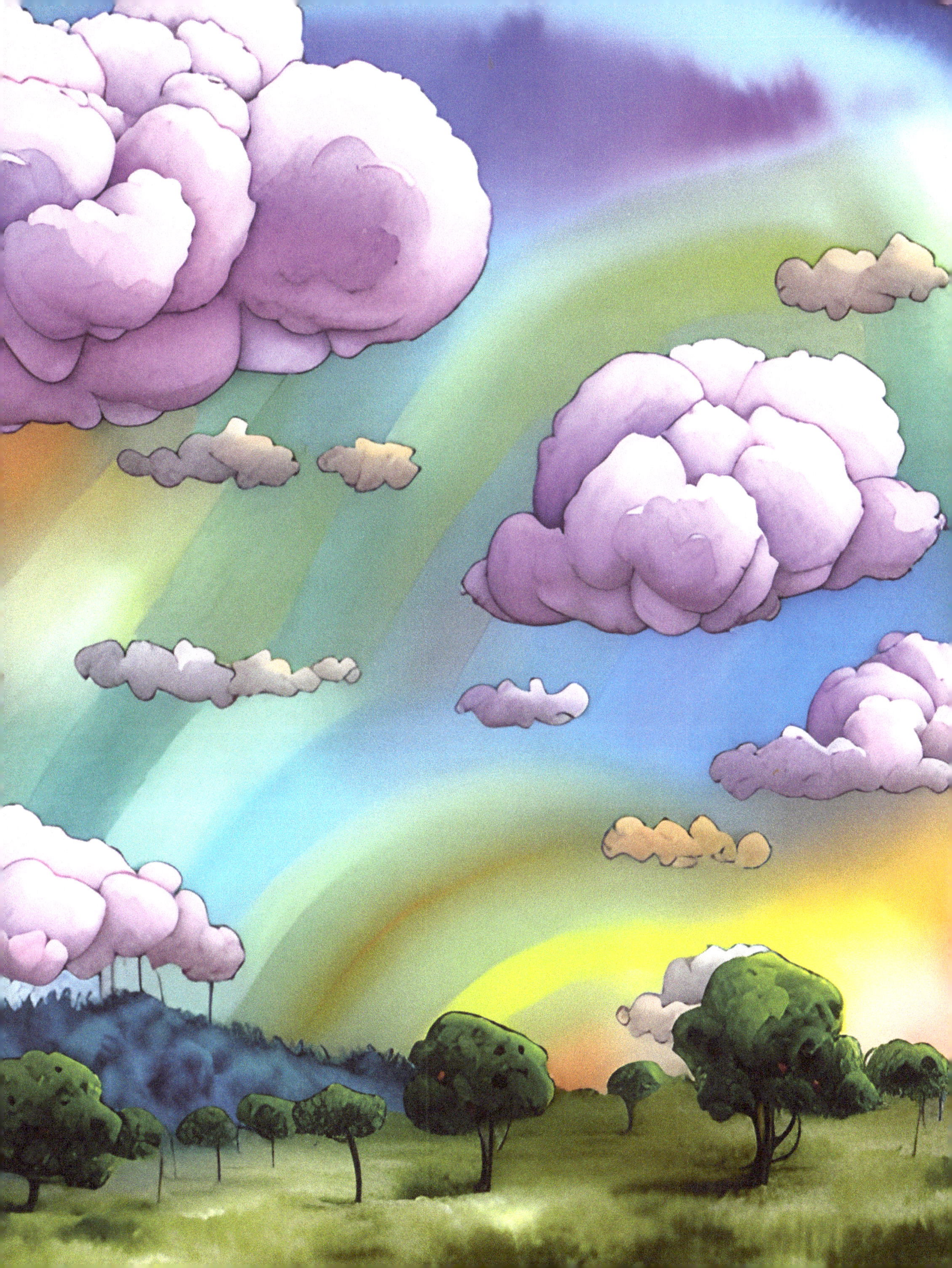

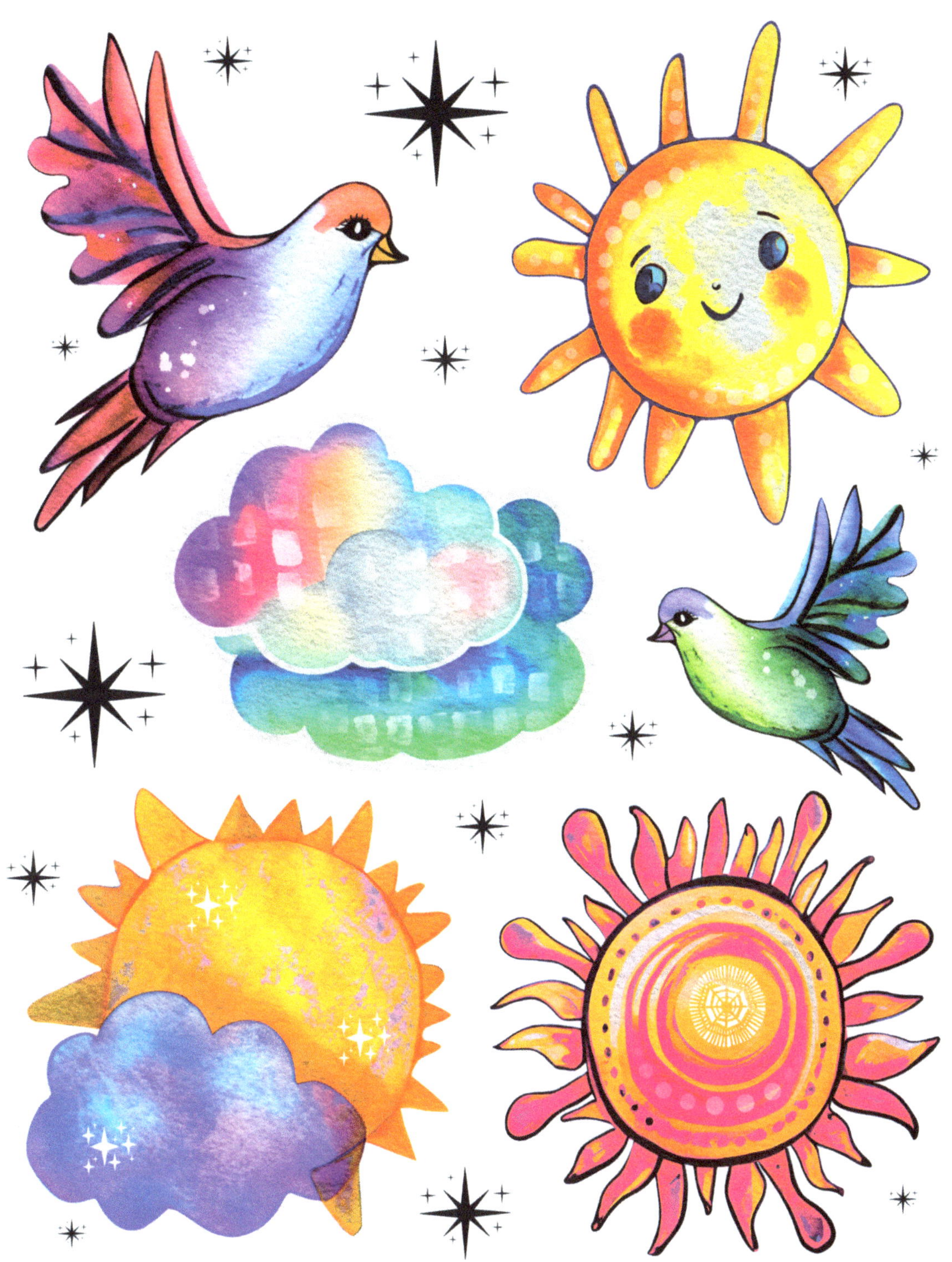

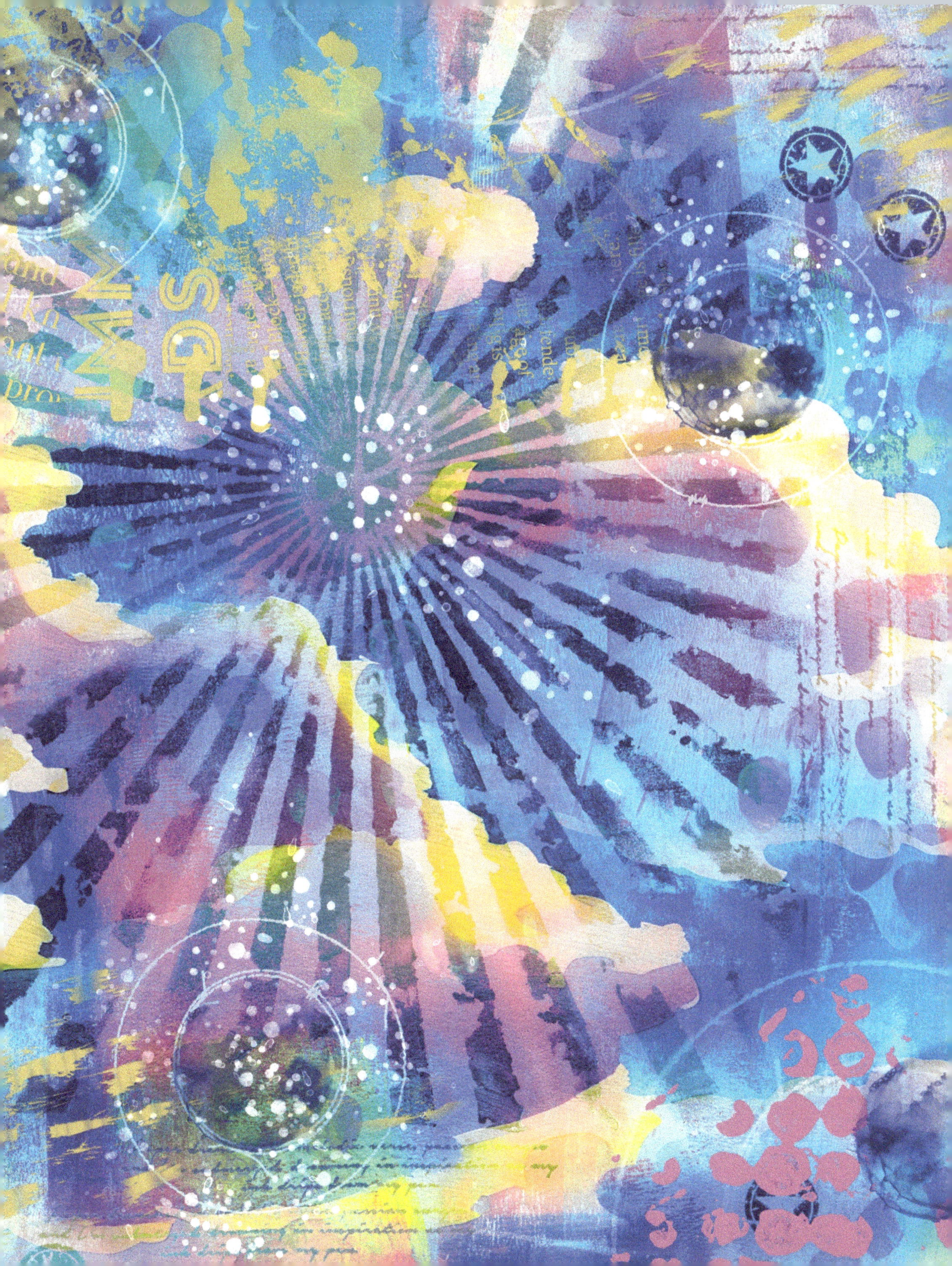

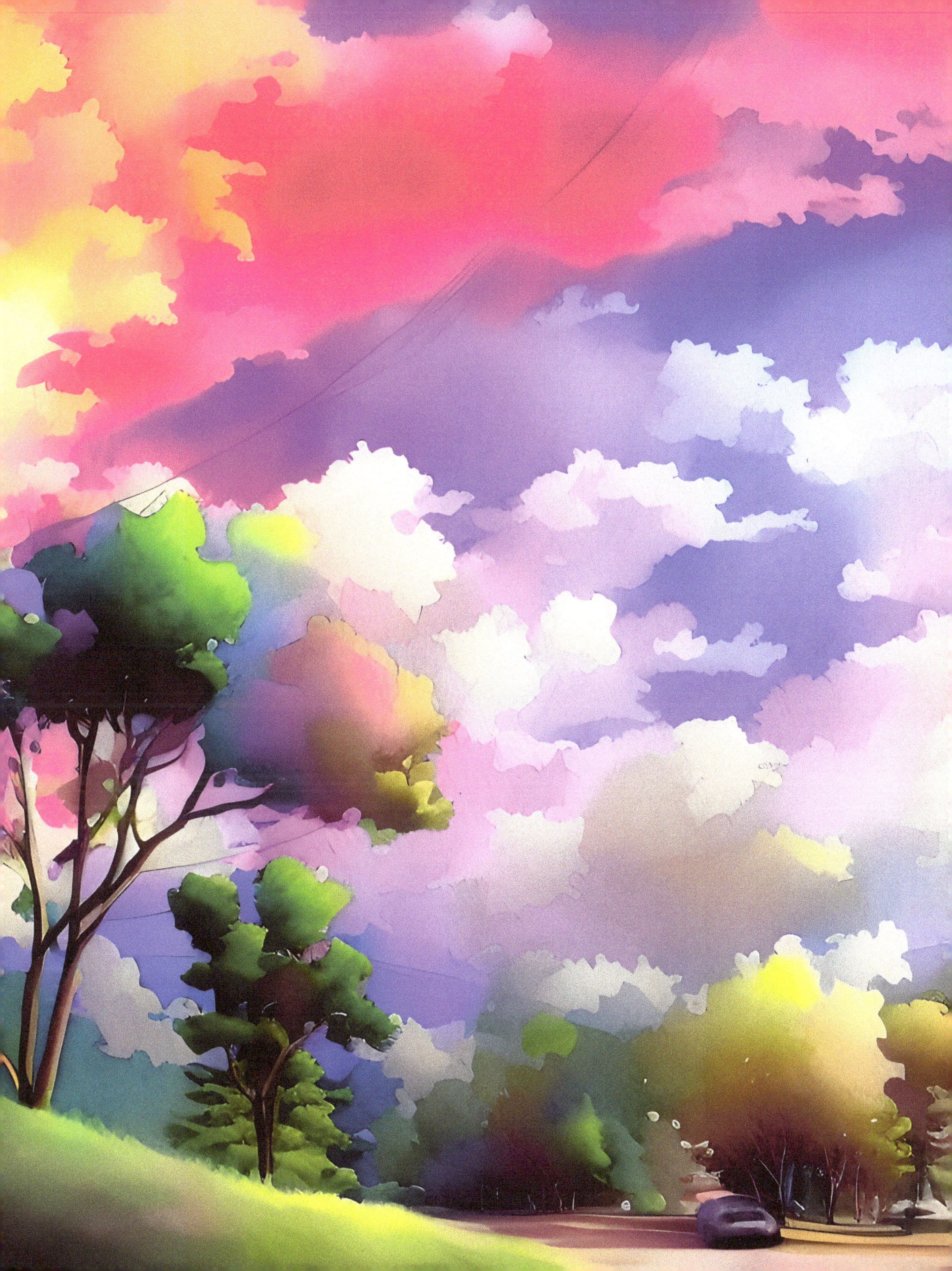

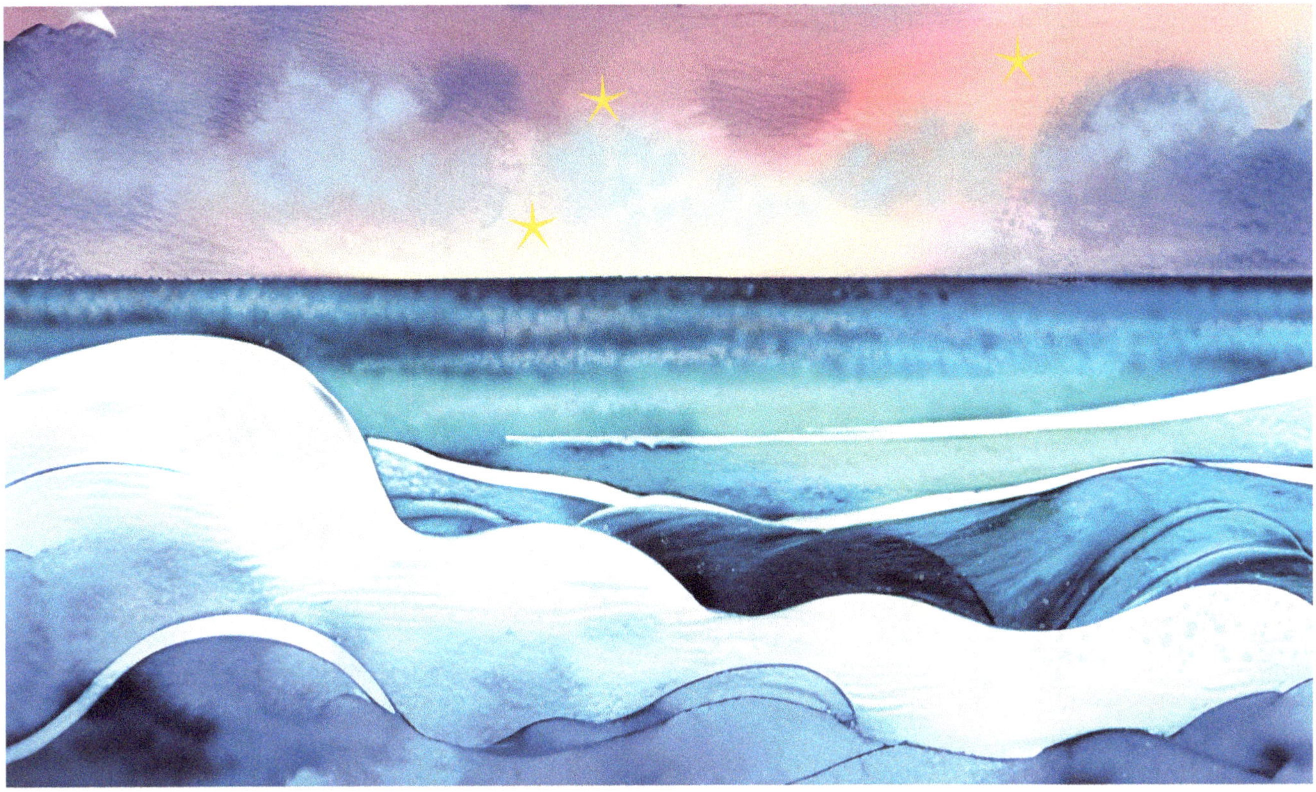

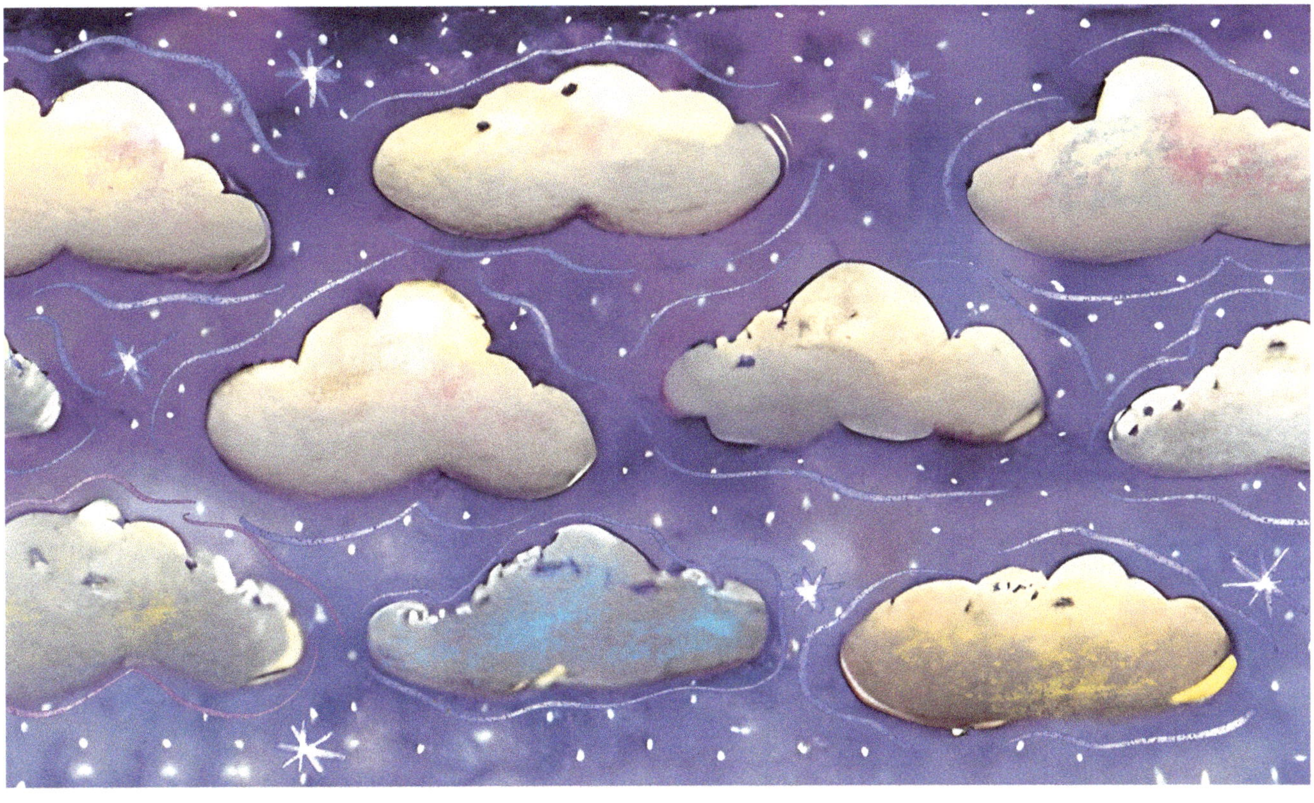

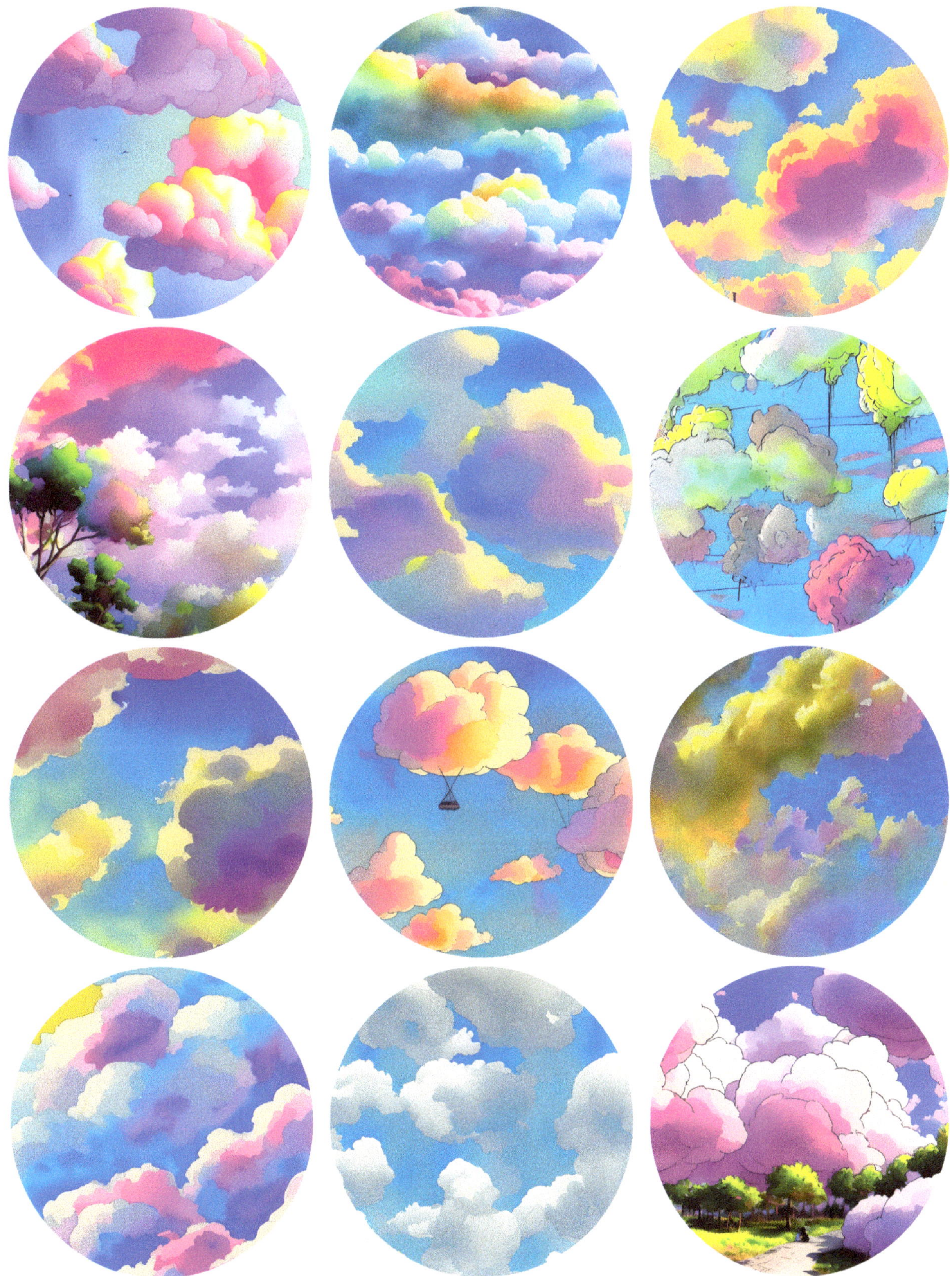

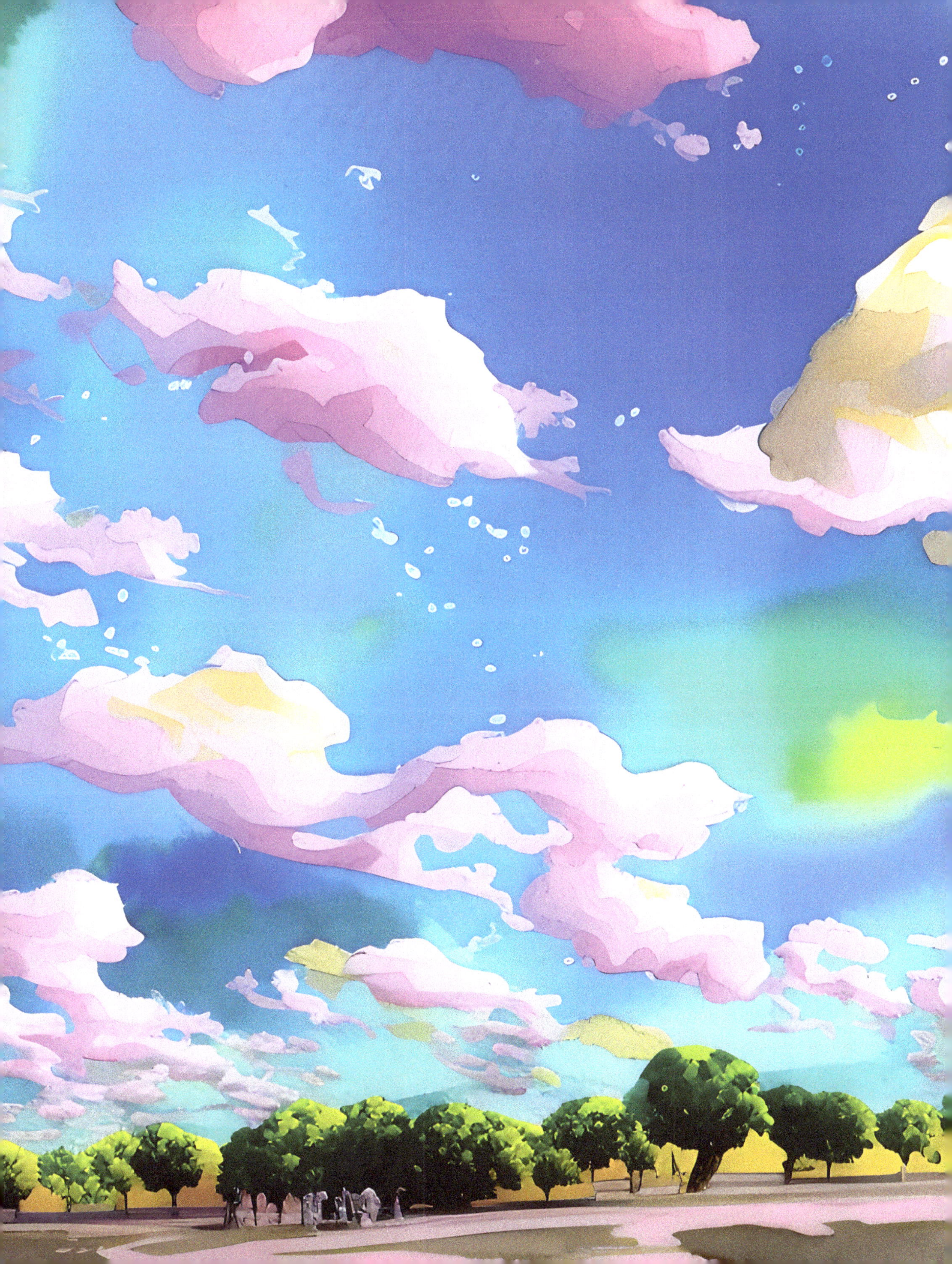

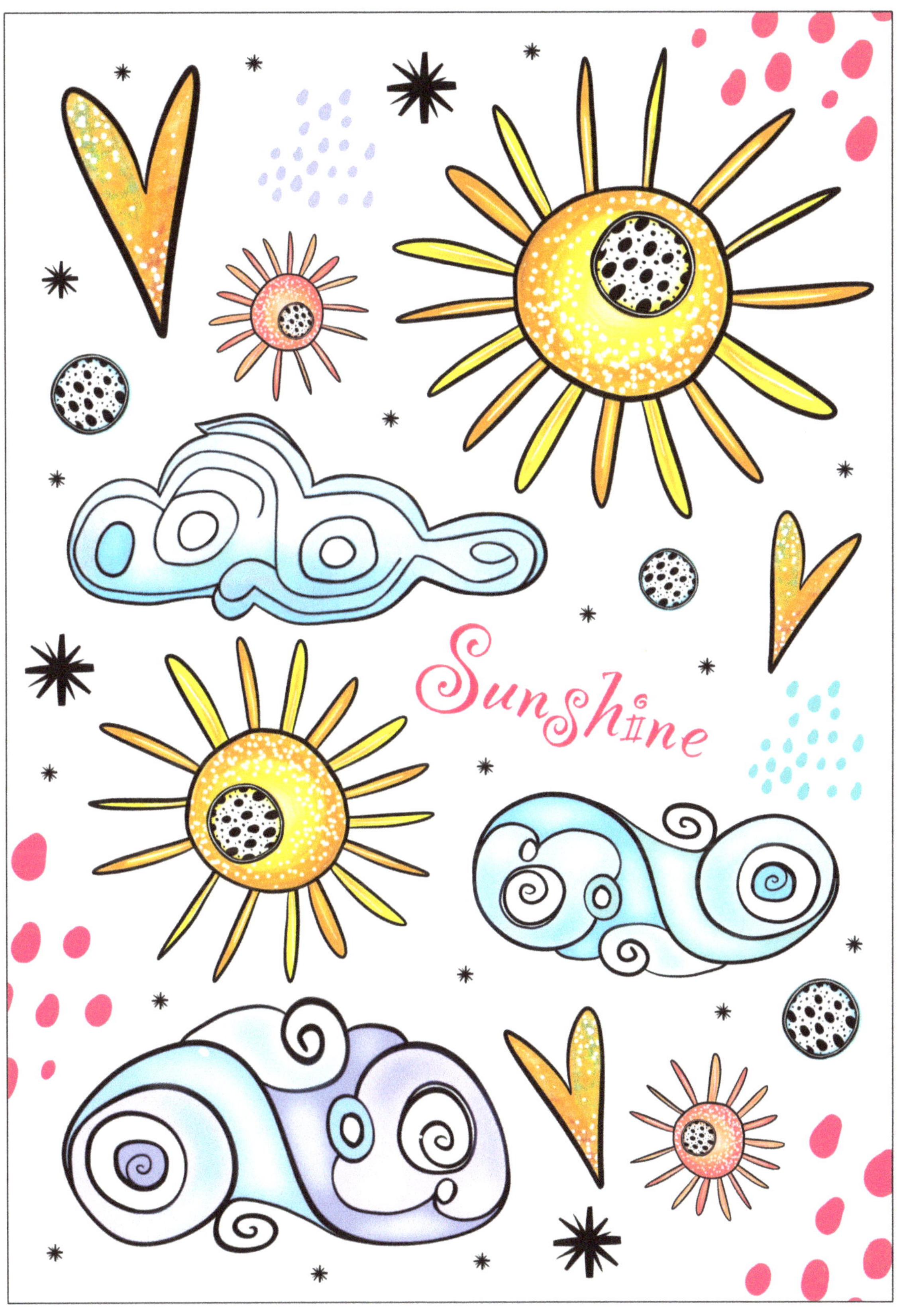
Sunshine

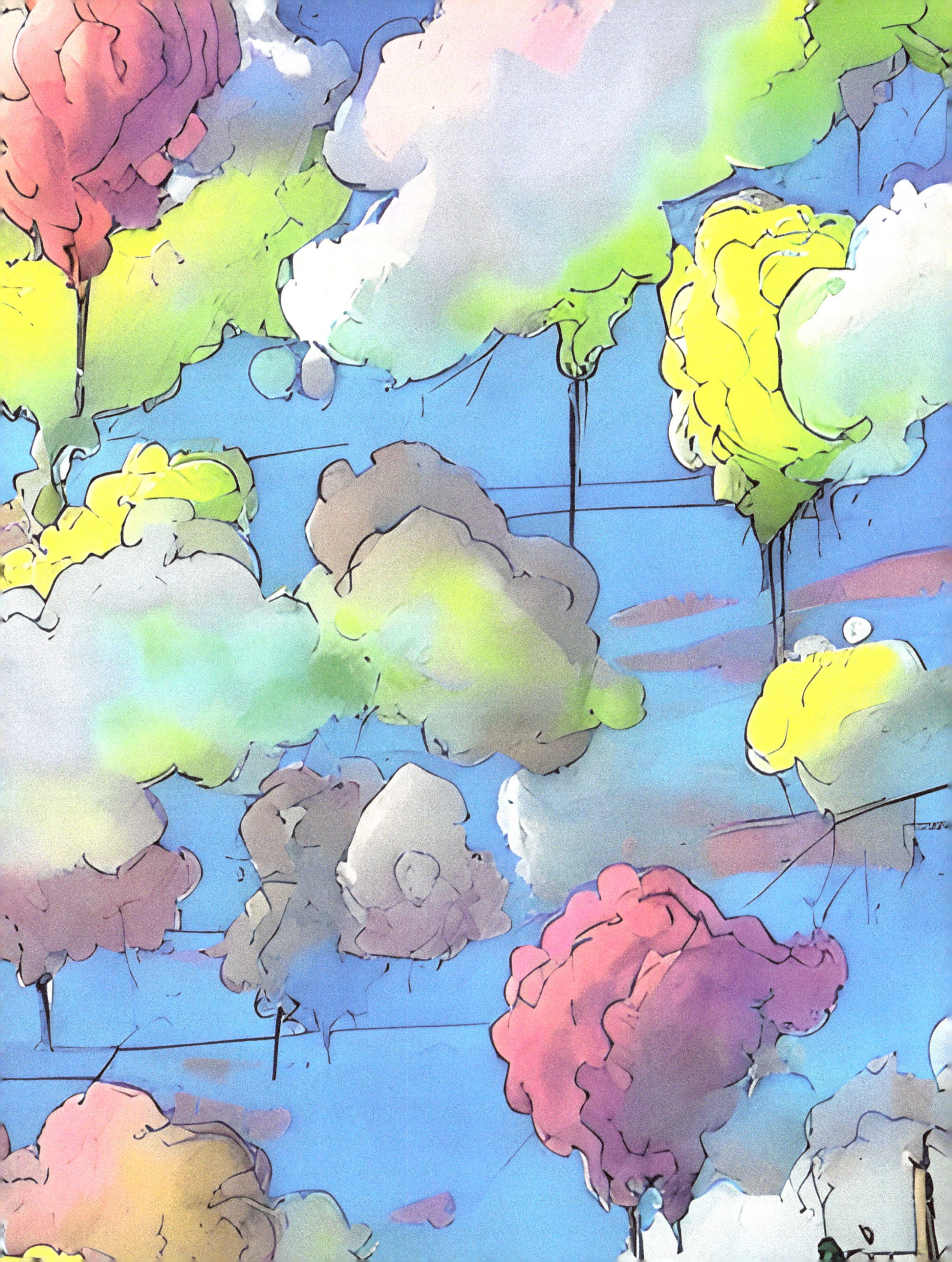

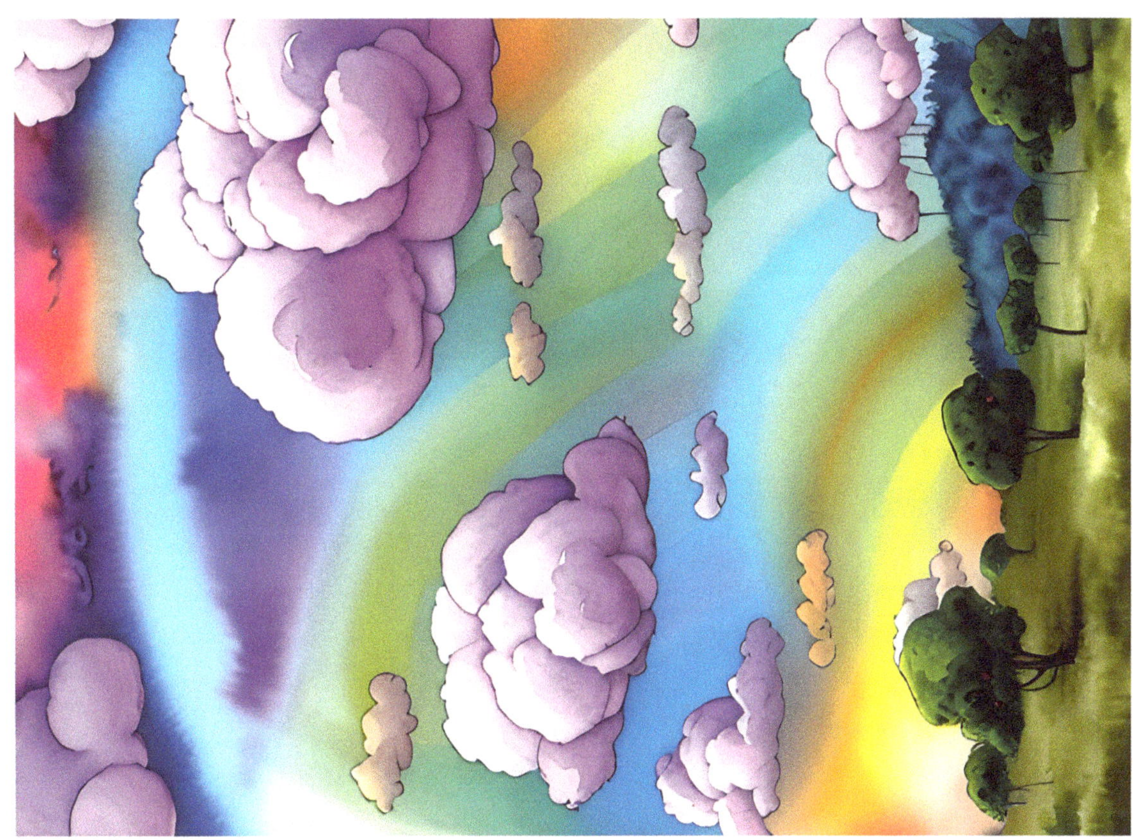

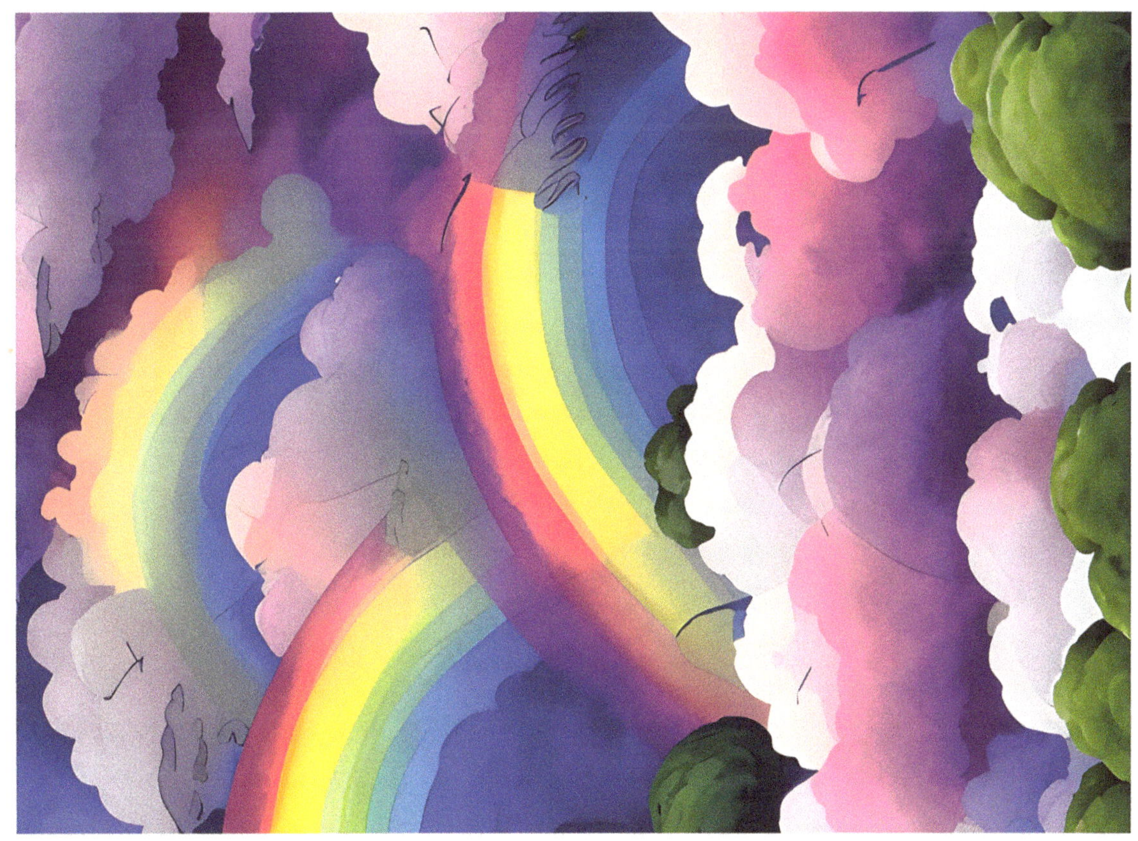

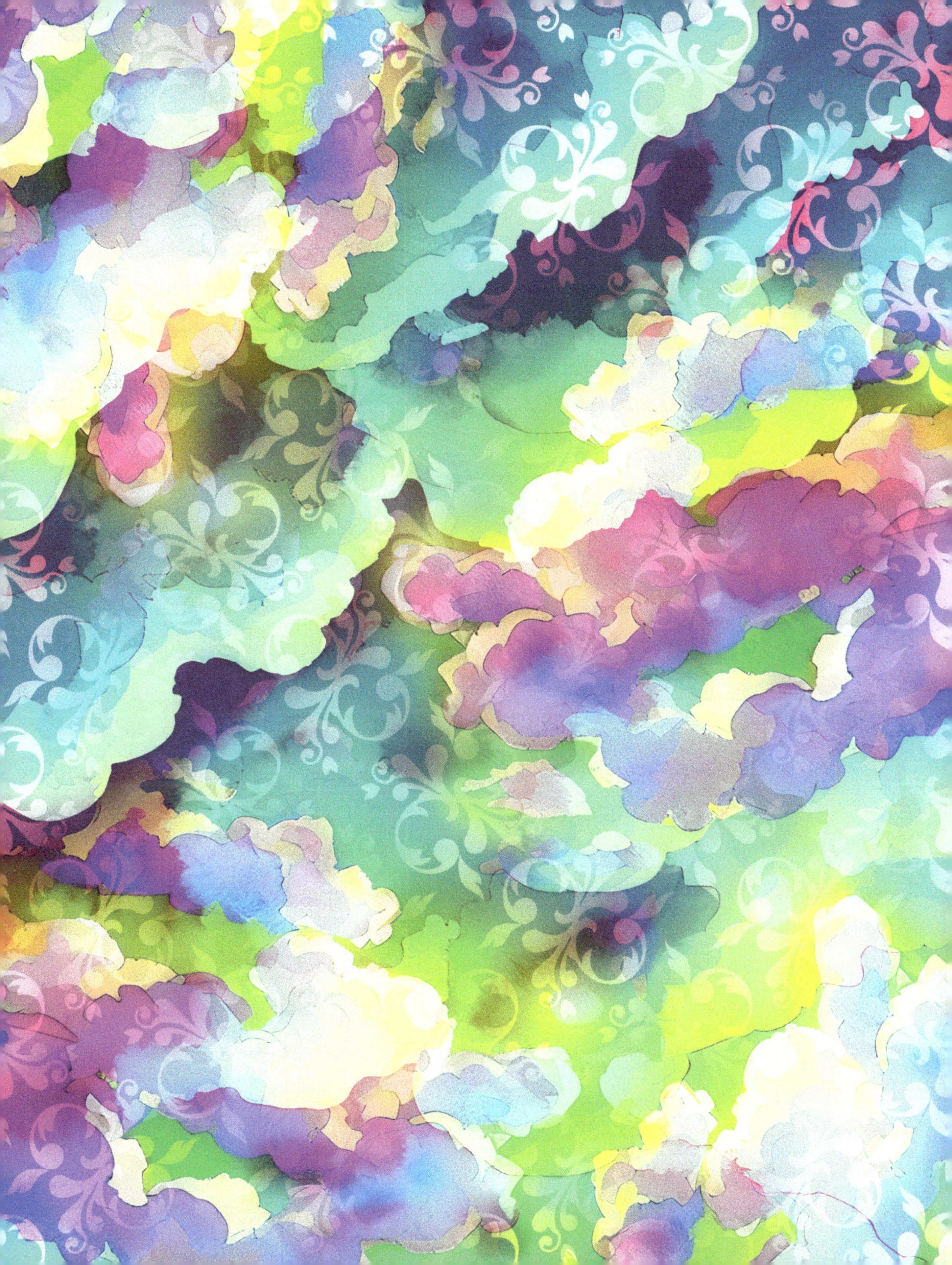

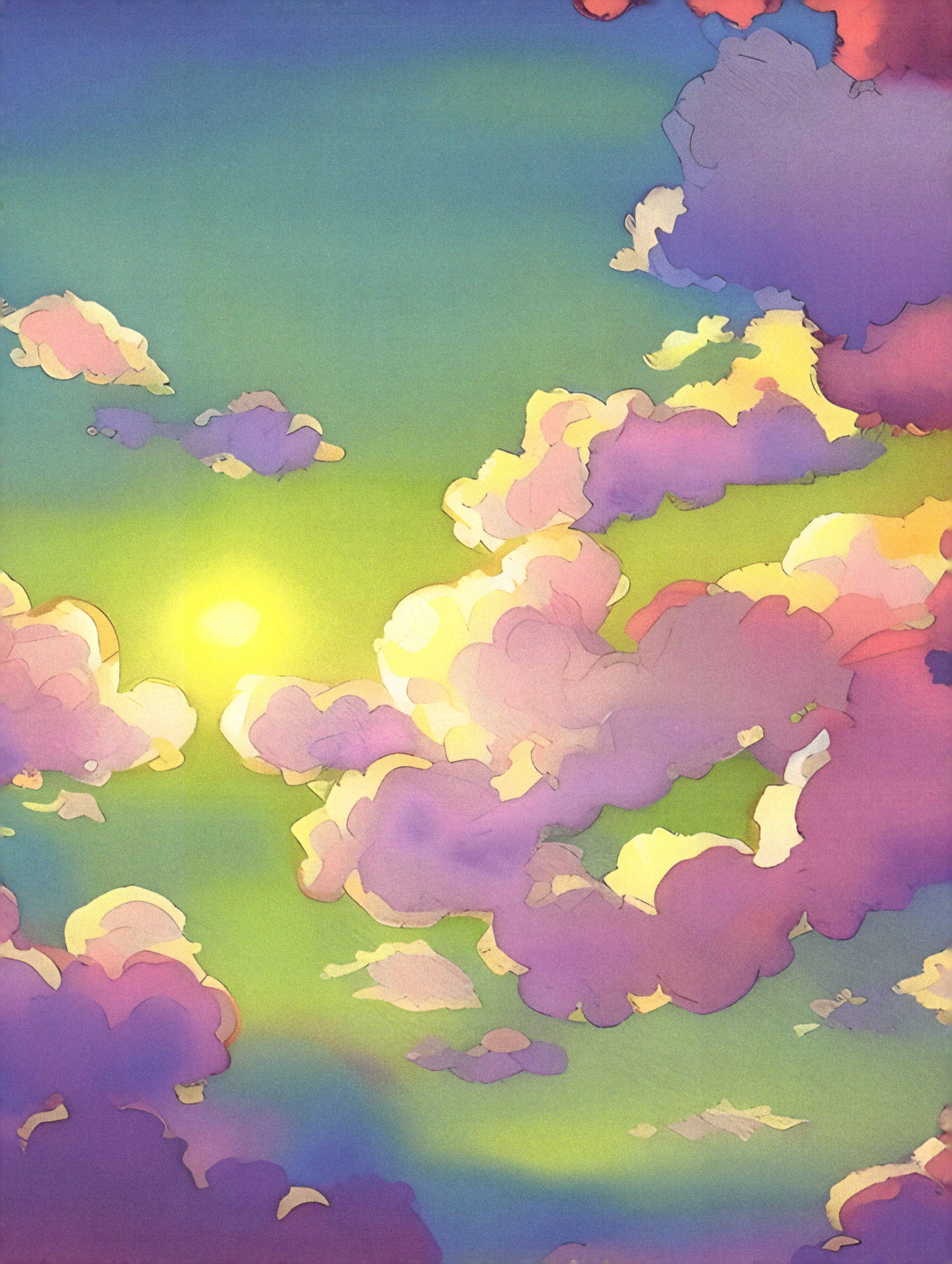

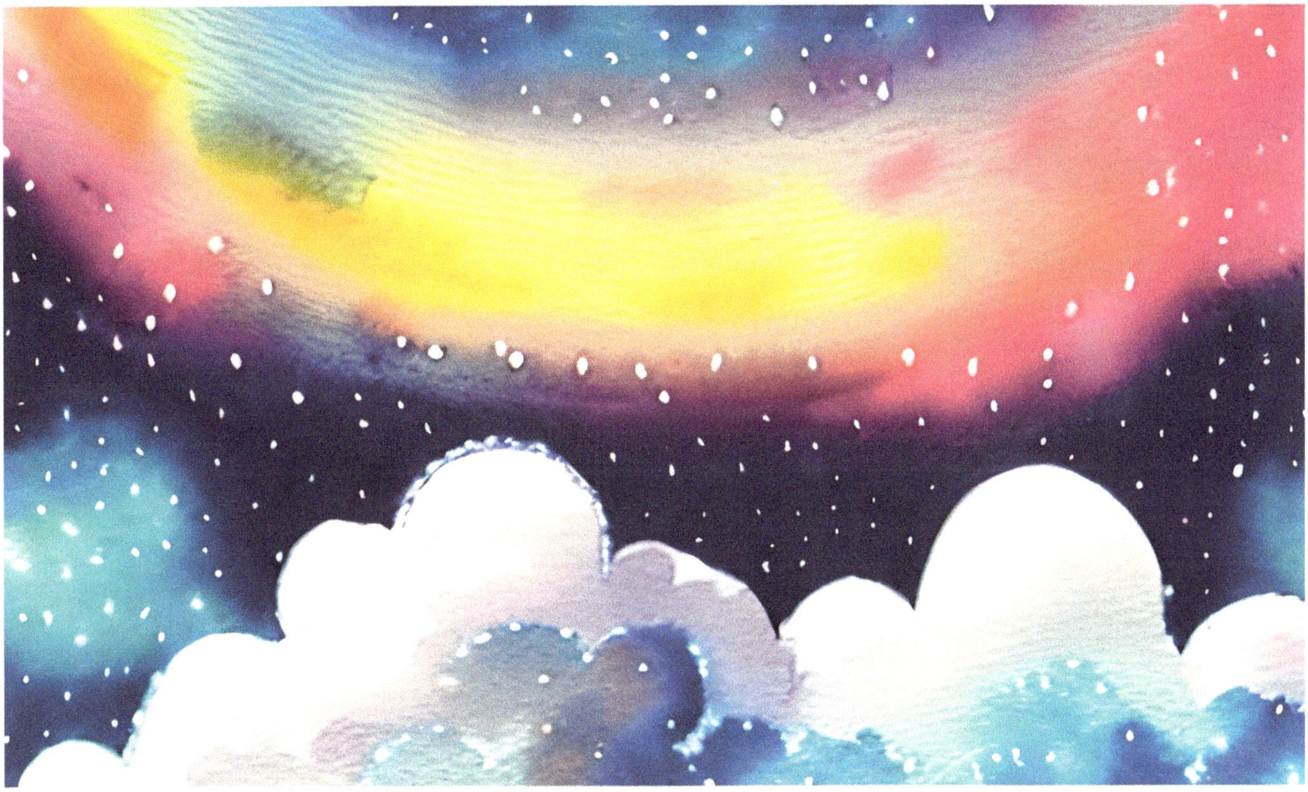

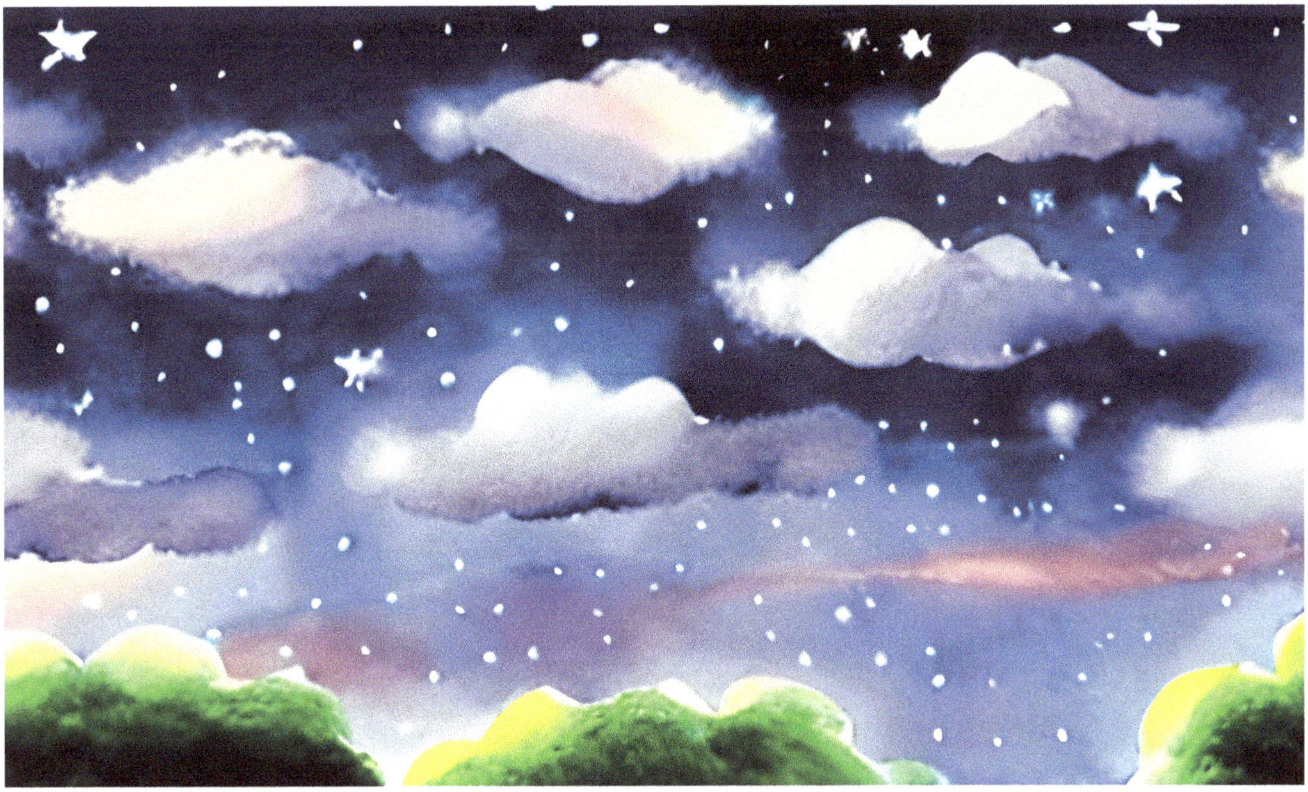

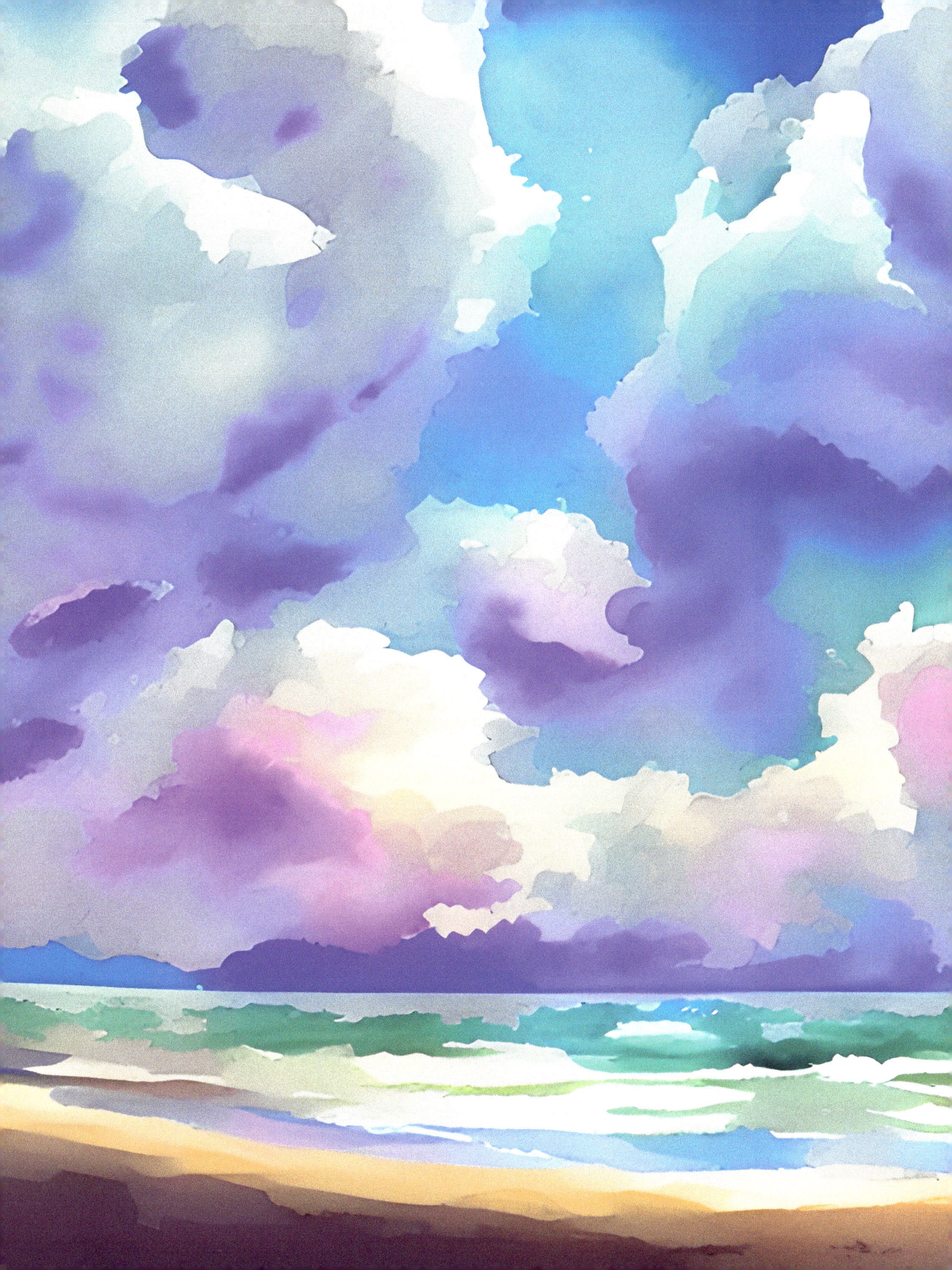

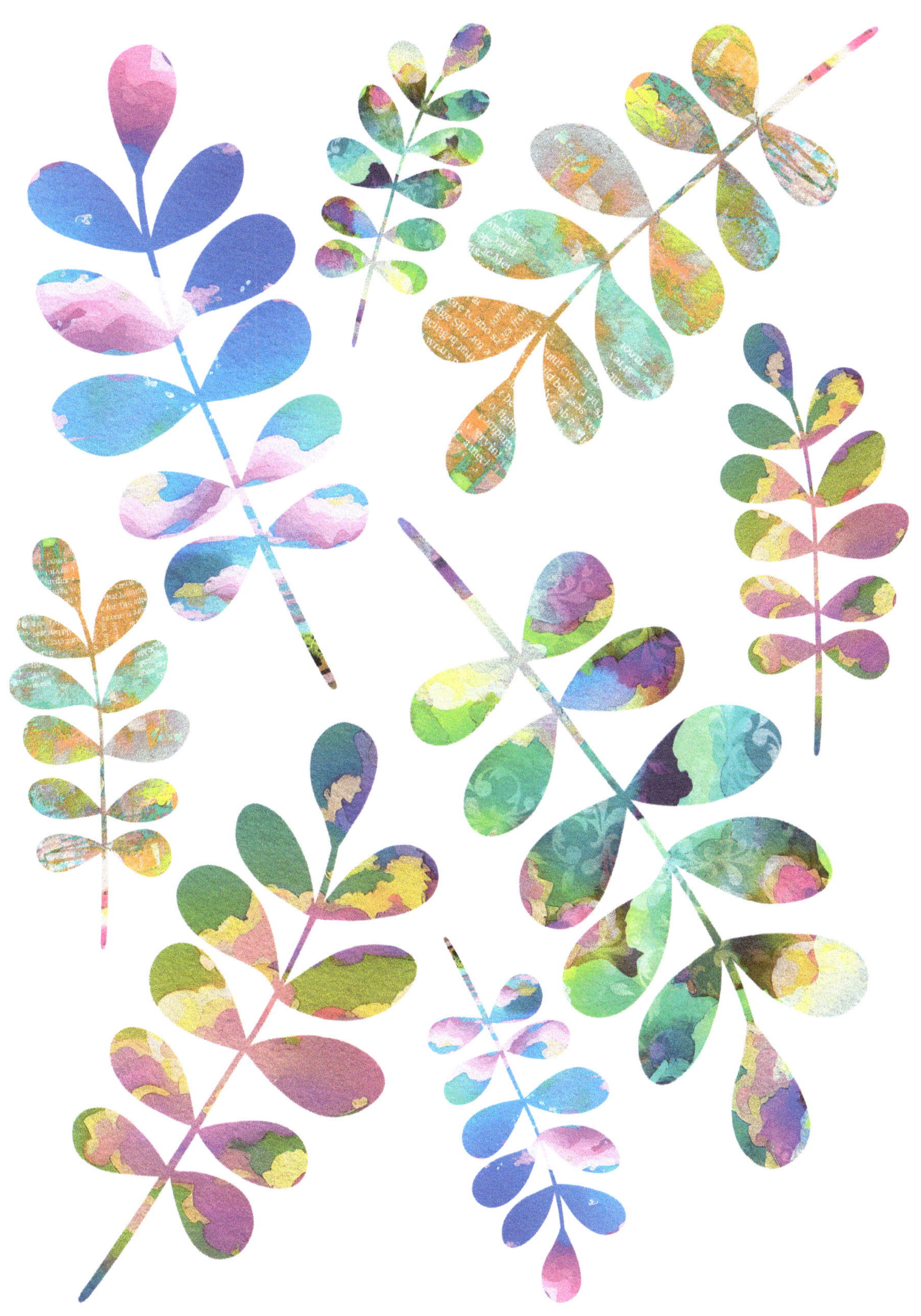

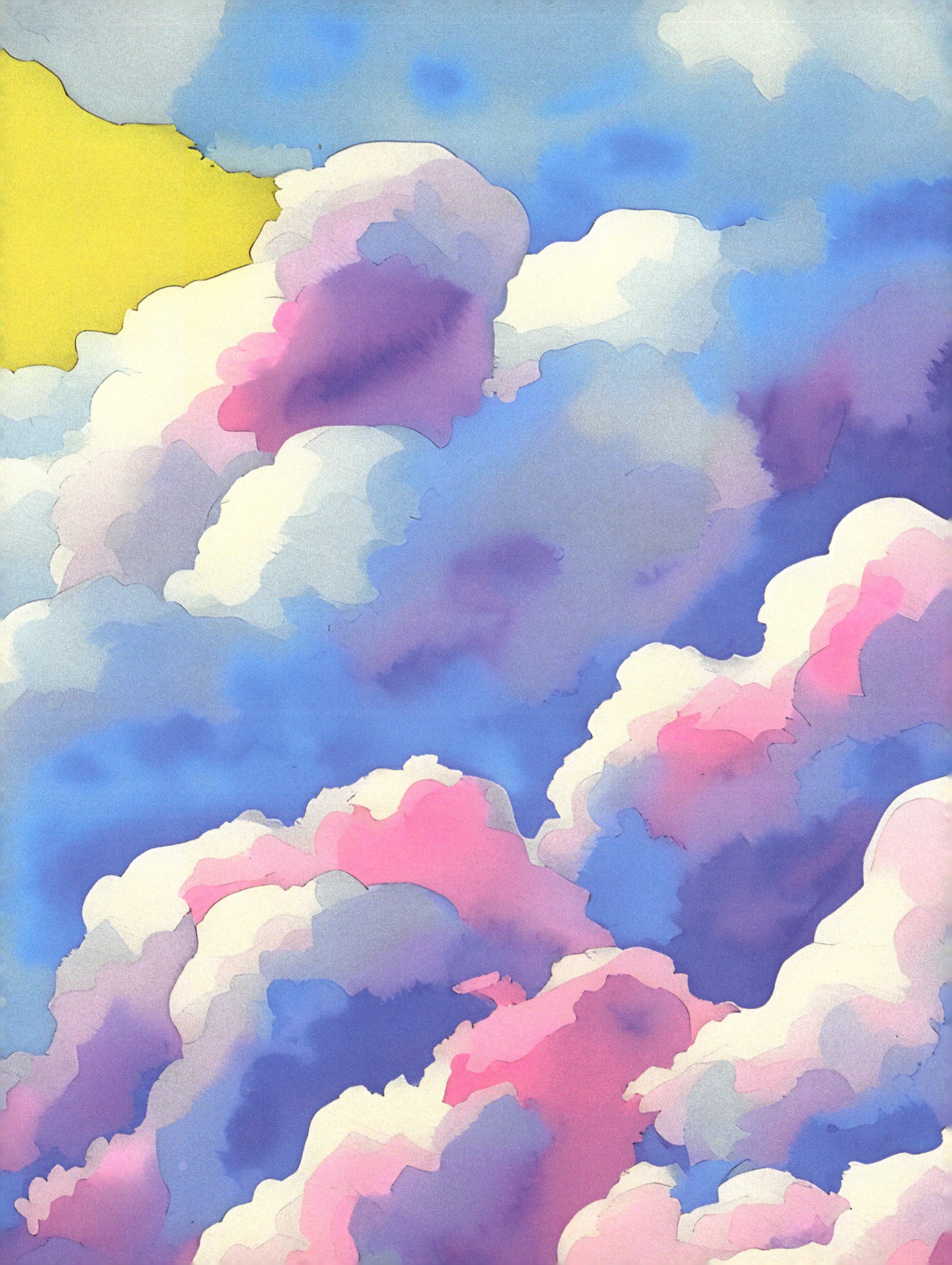

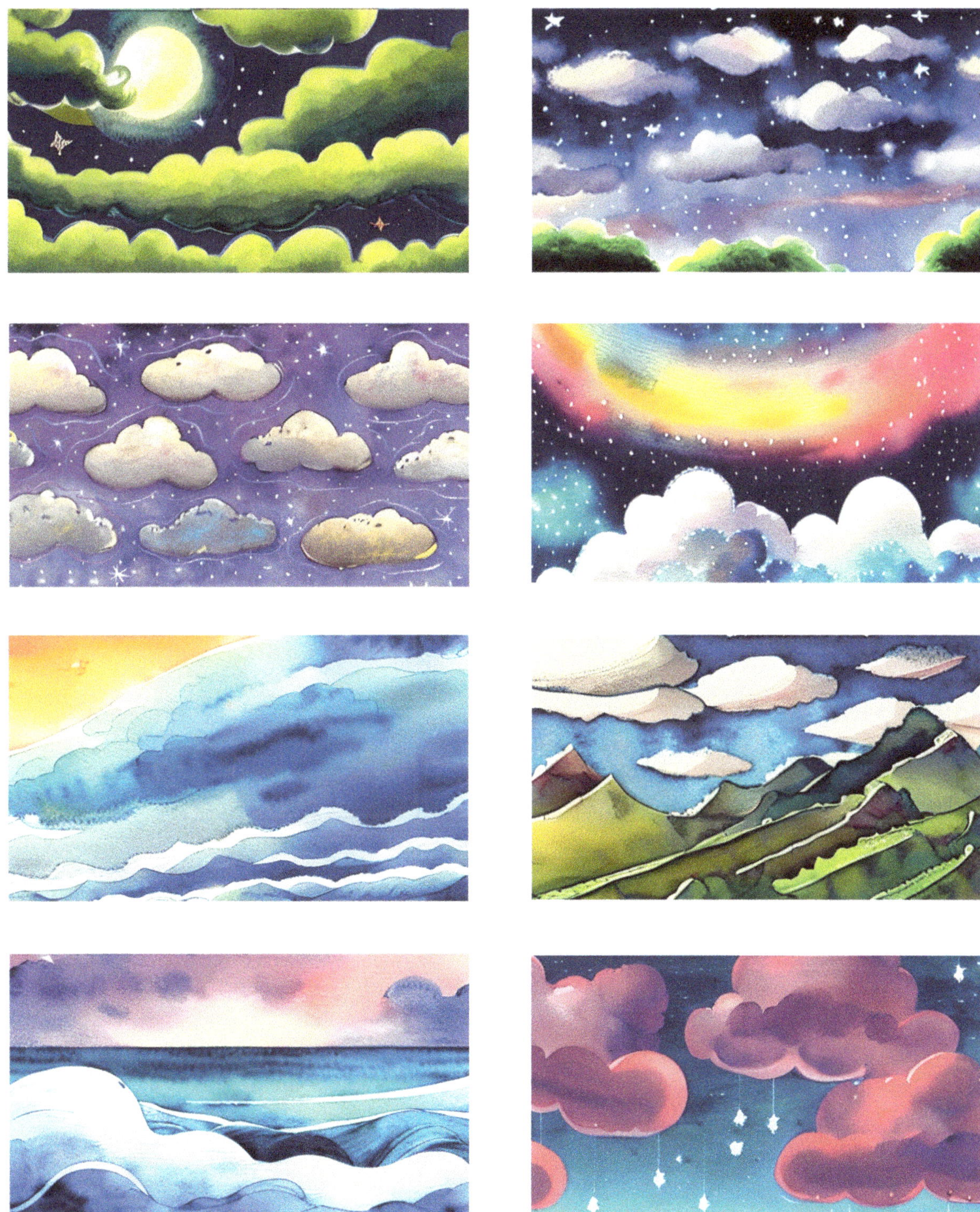

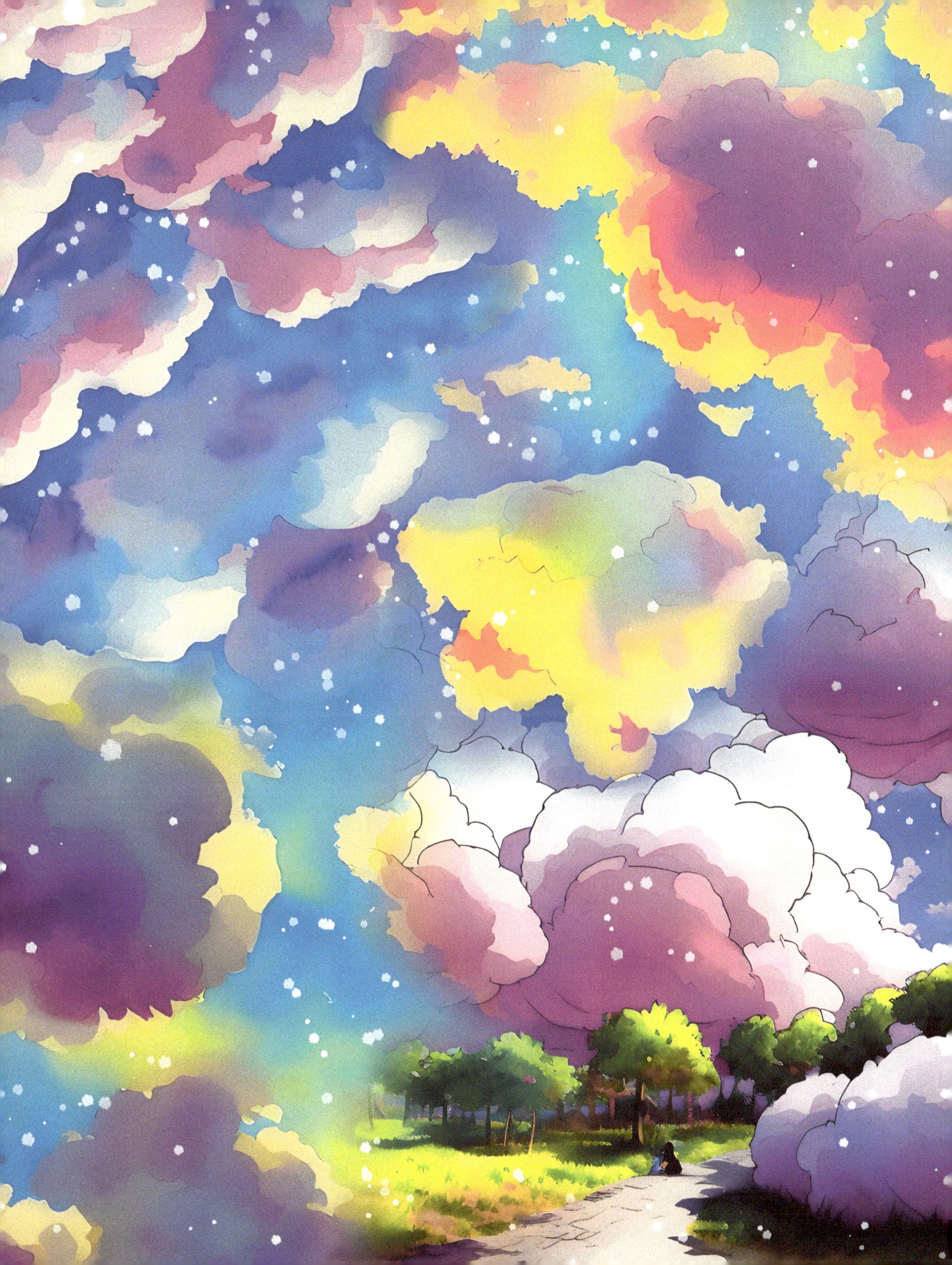

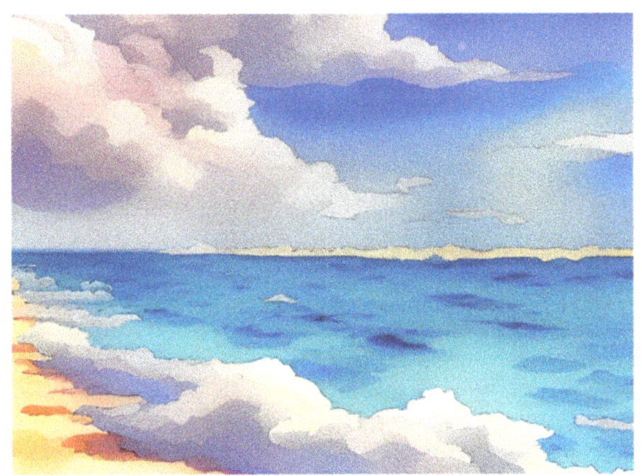
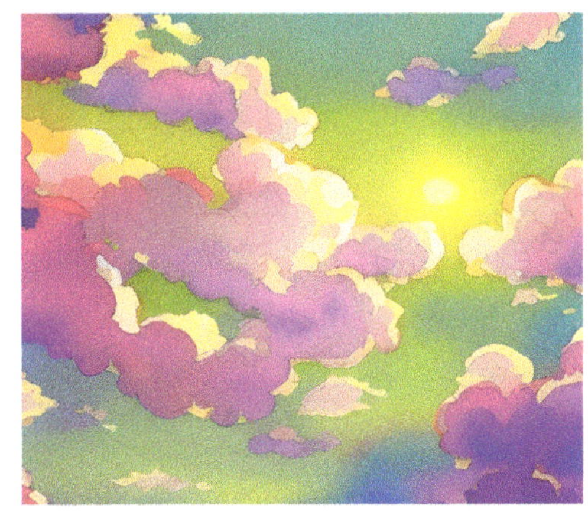
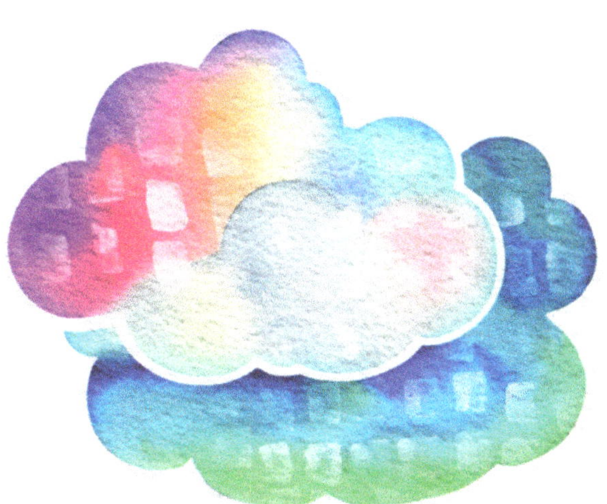
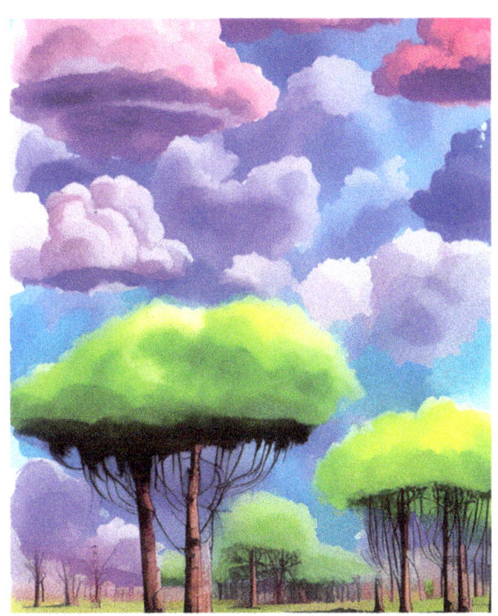
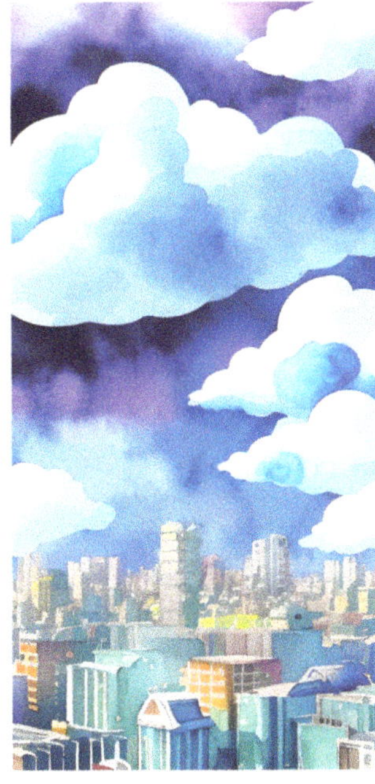
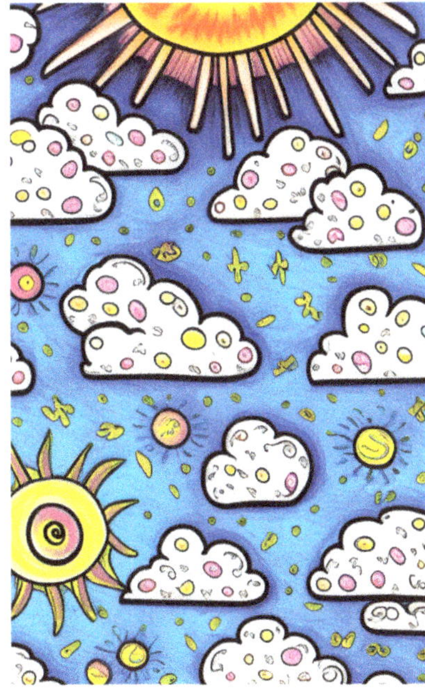
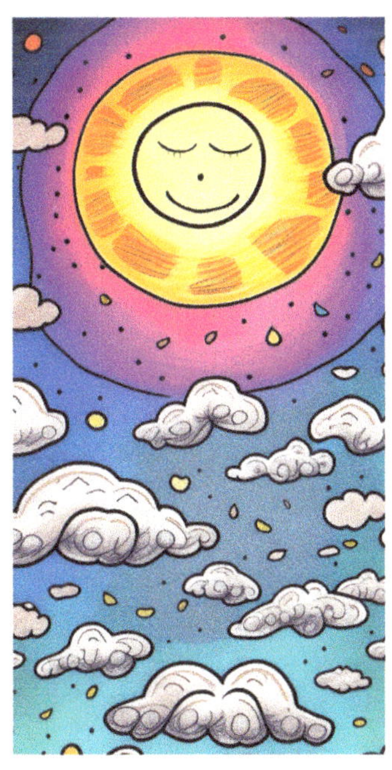

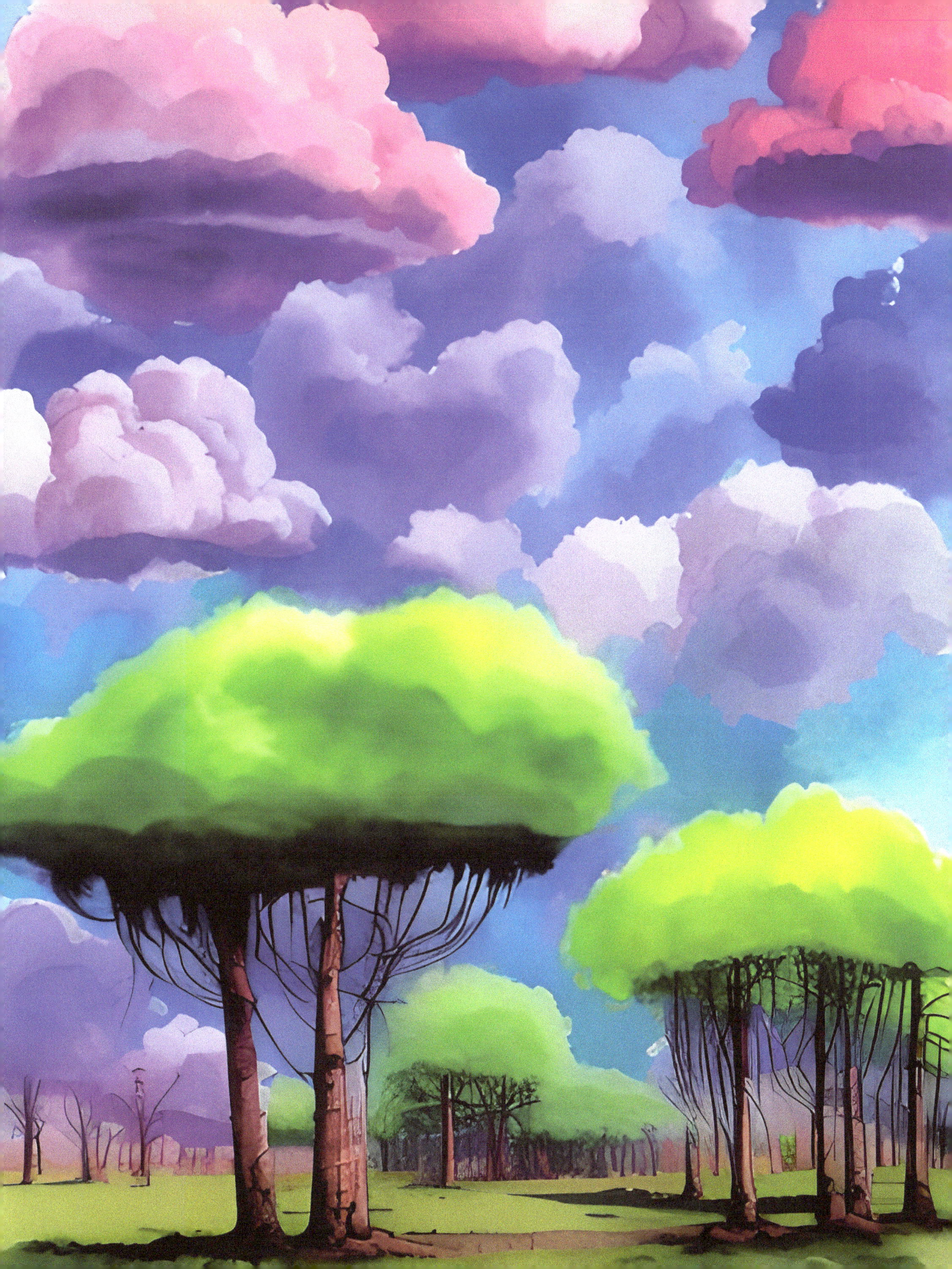

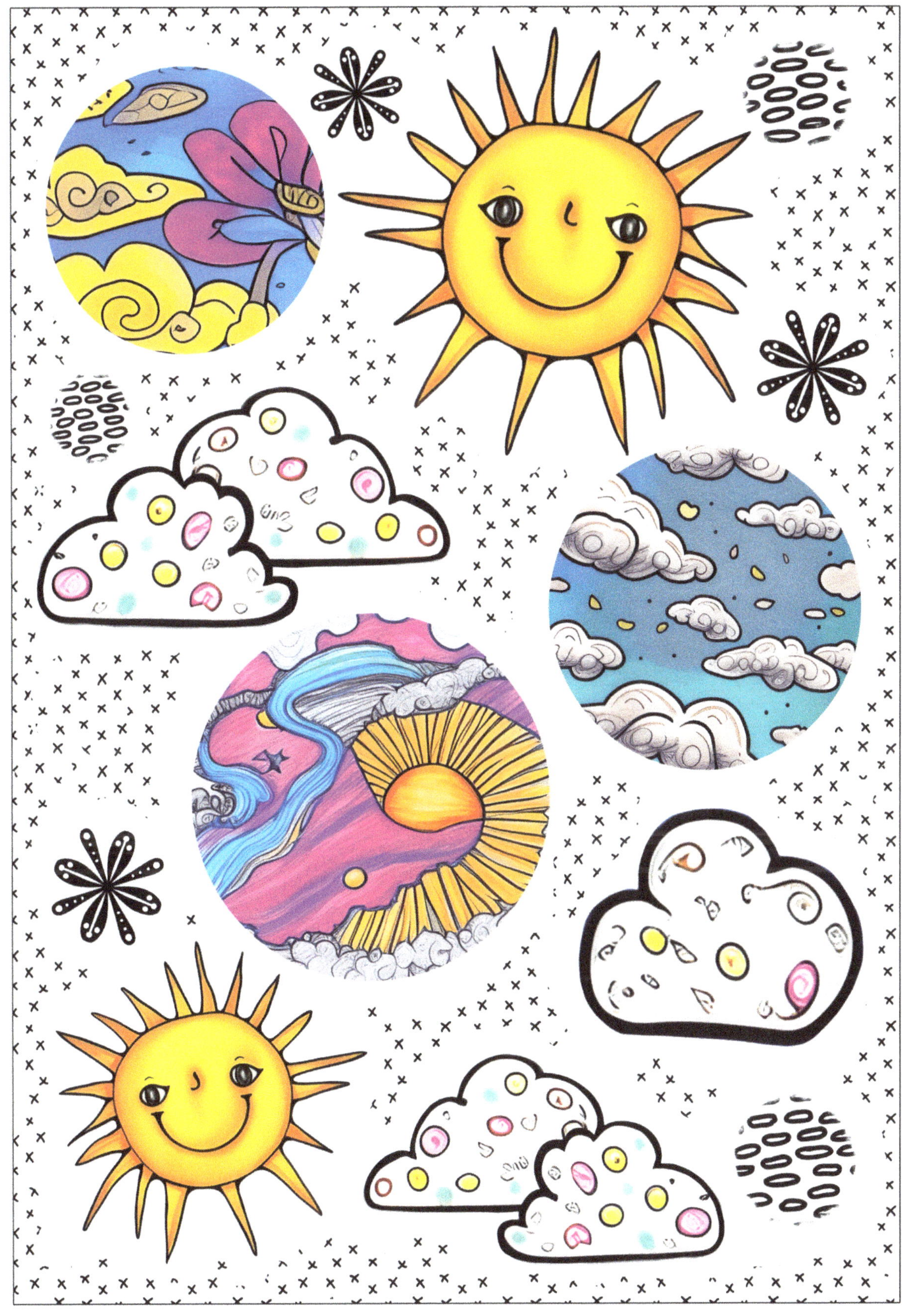

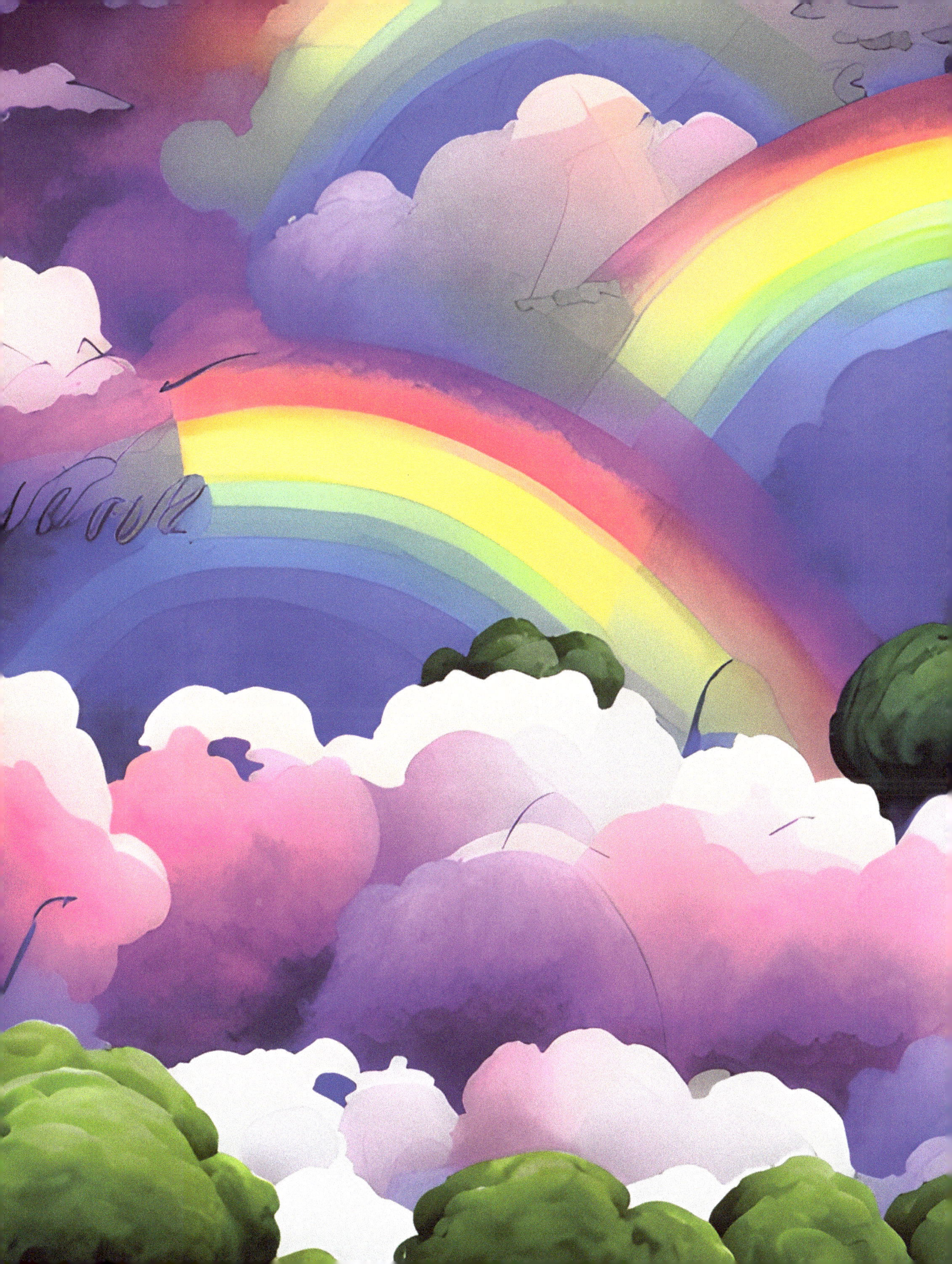

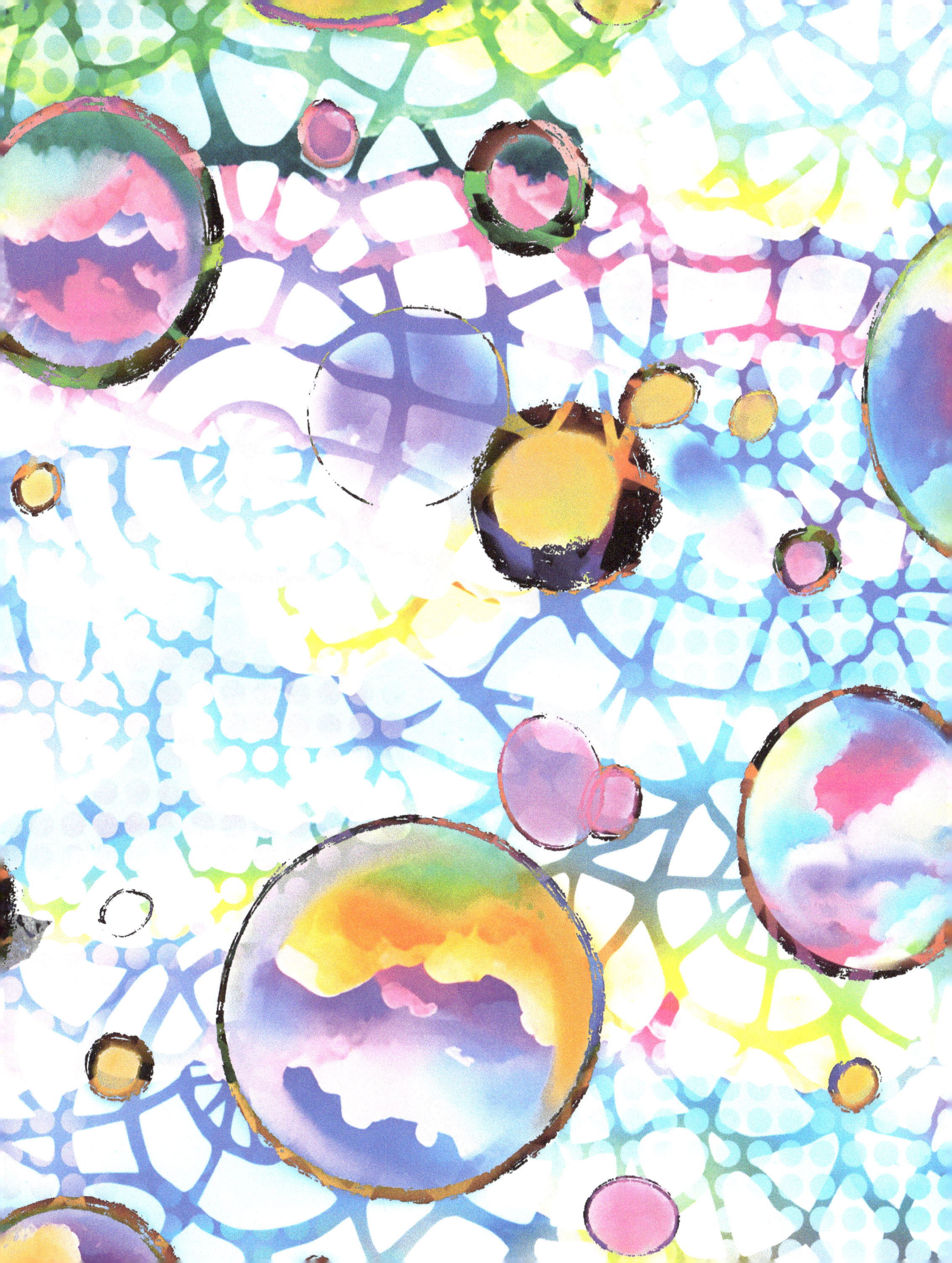

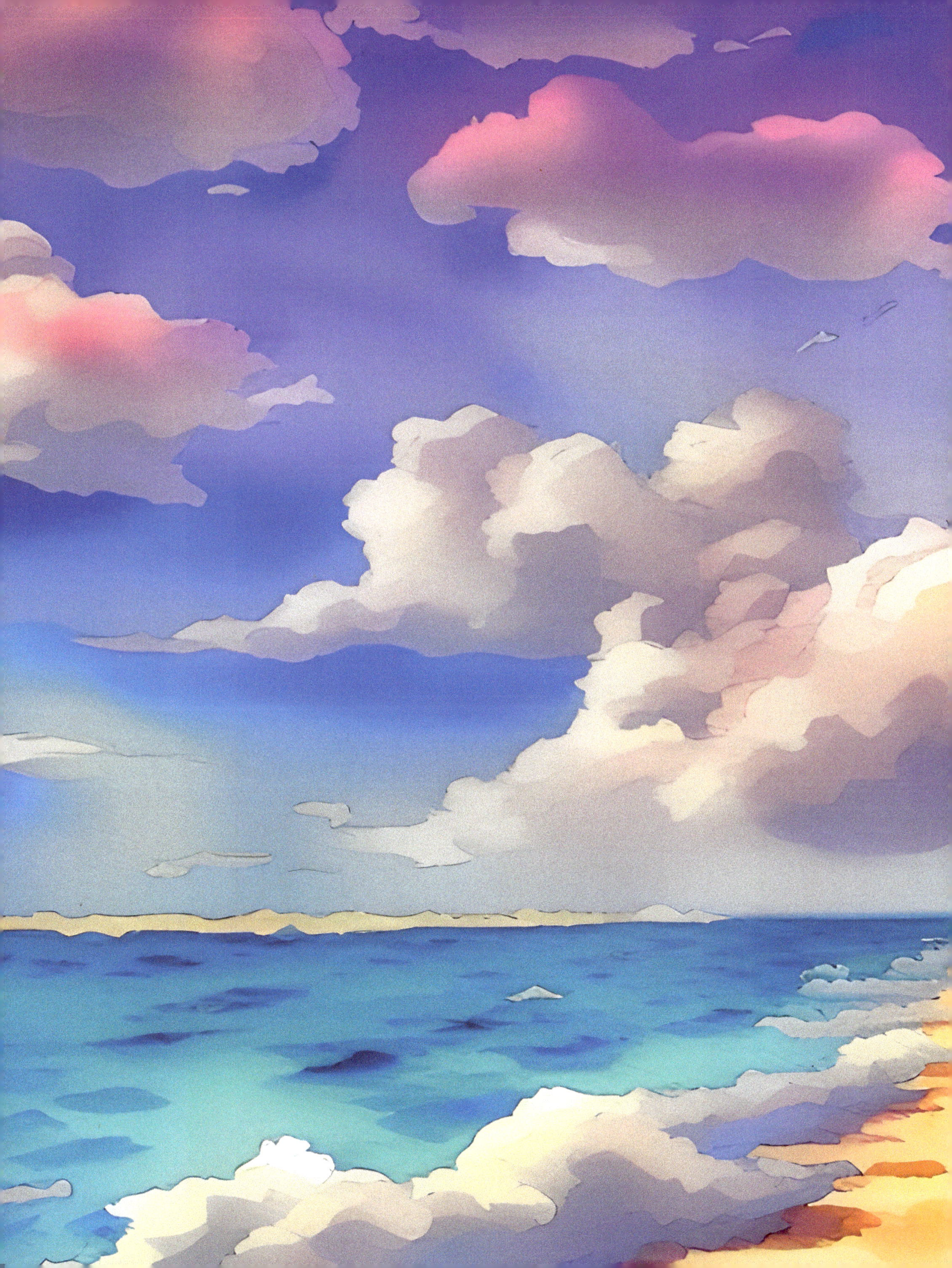

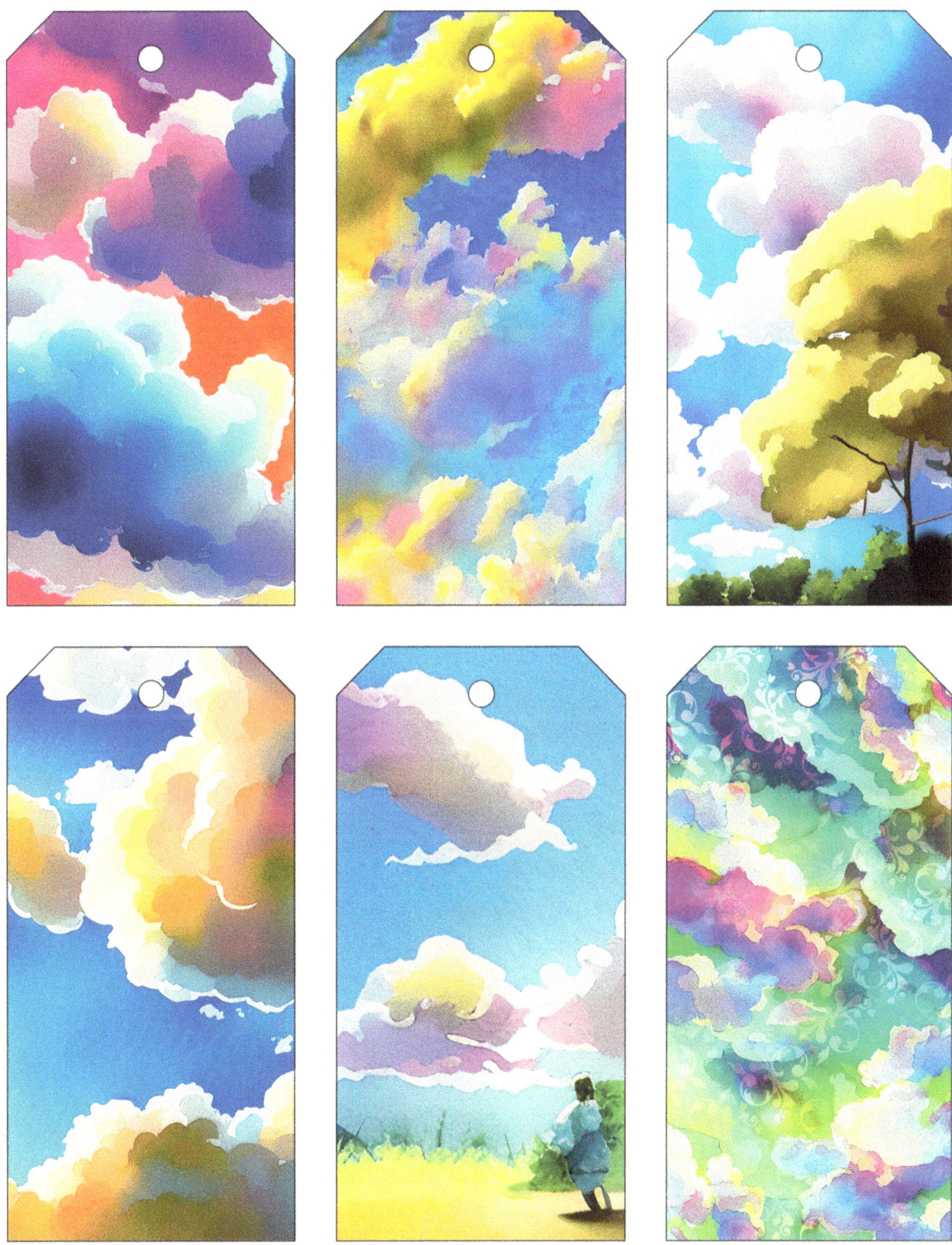

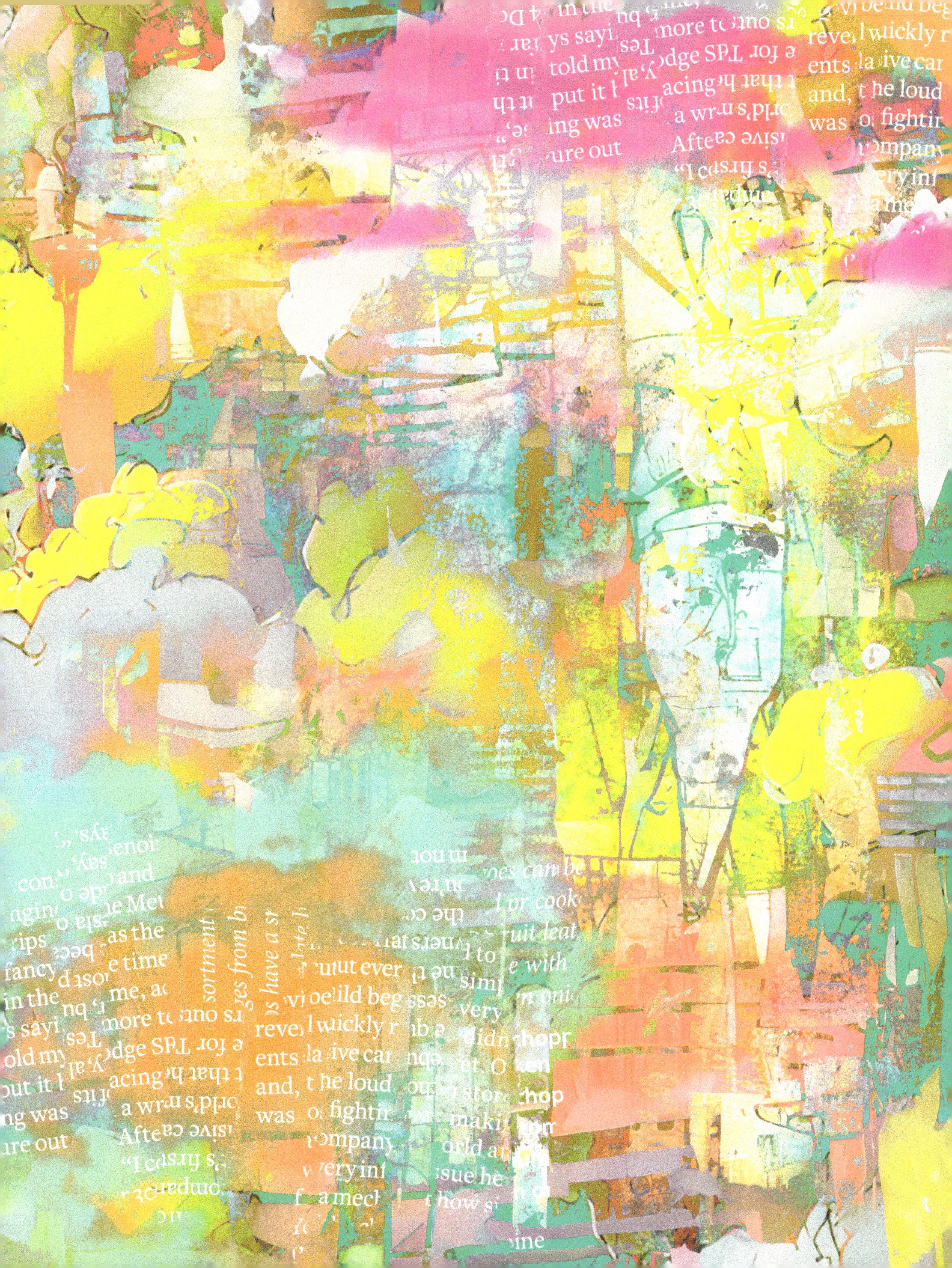

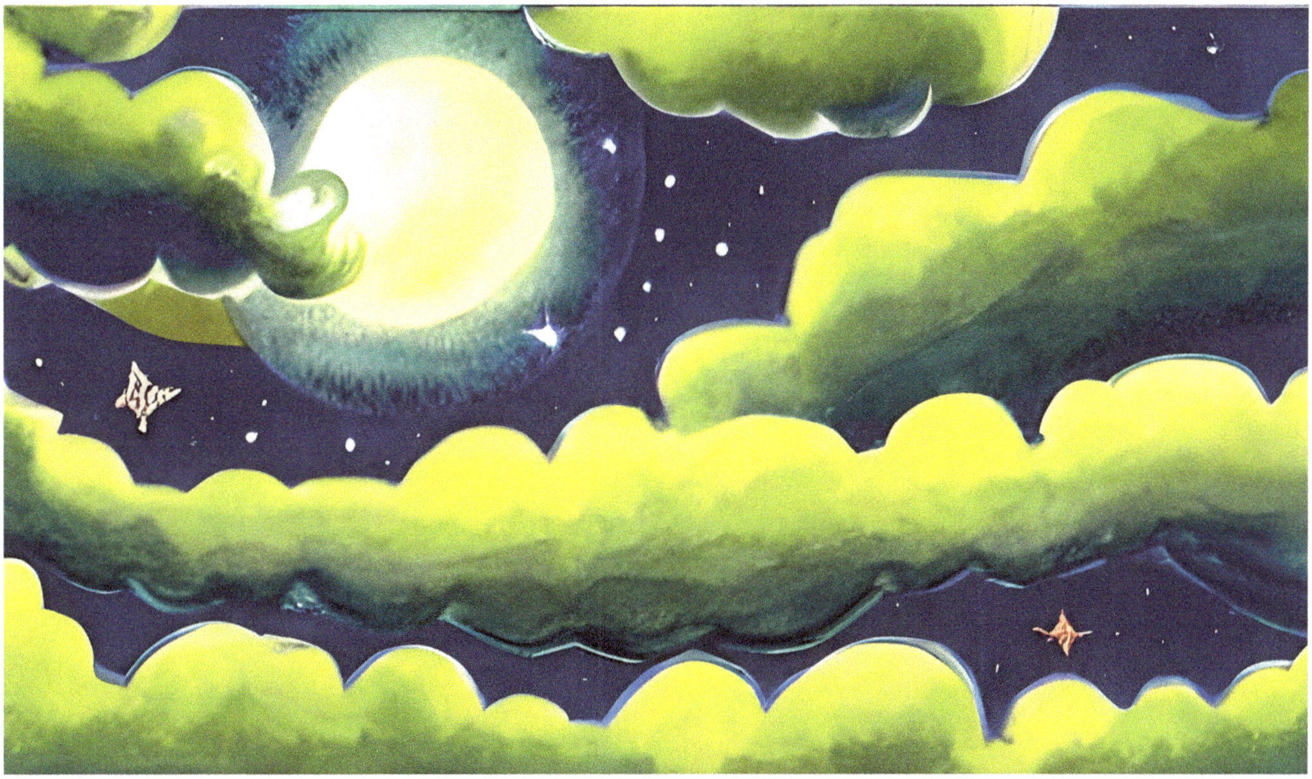

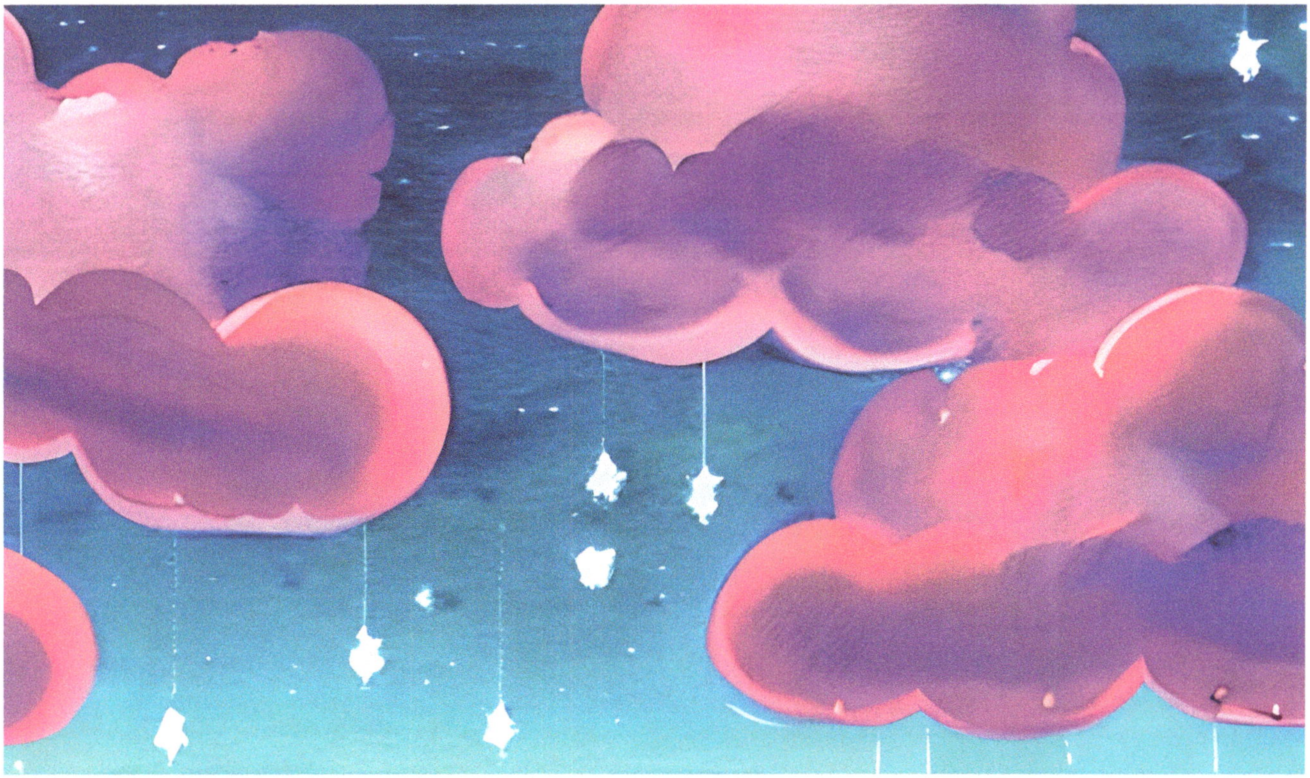

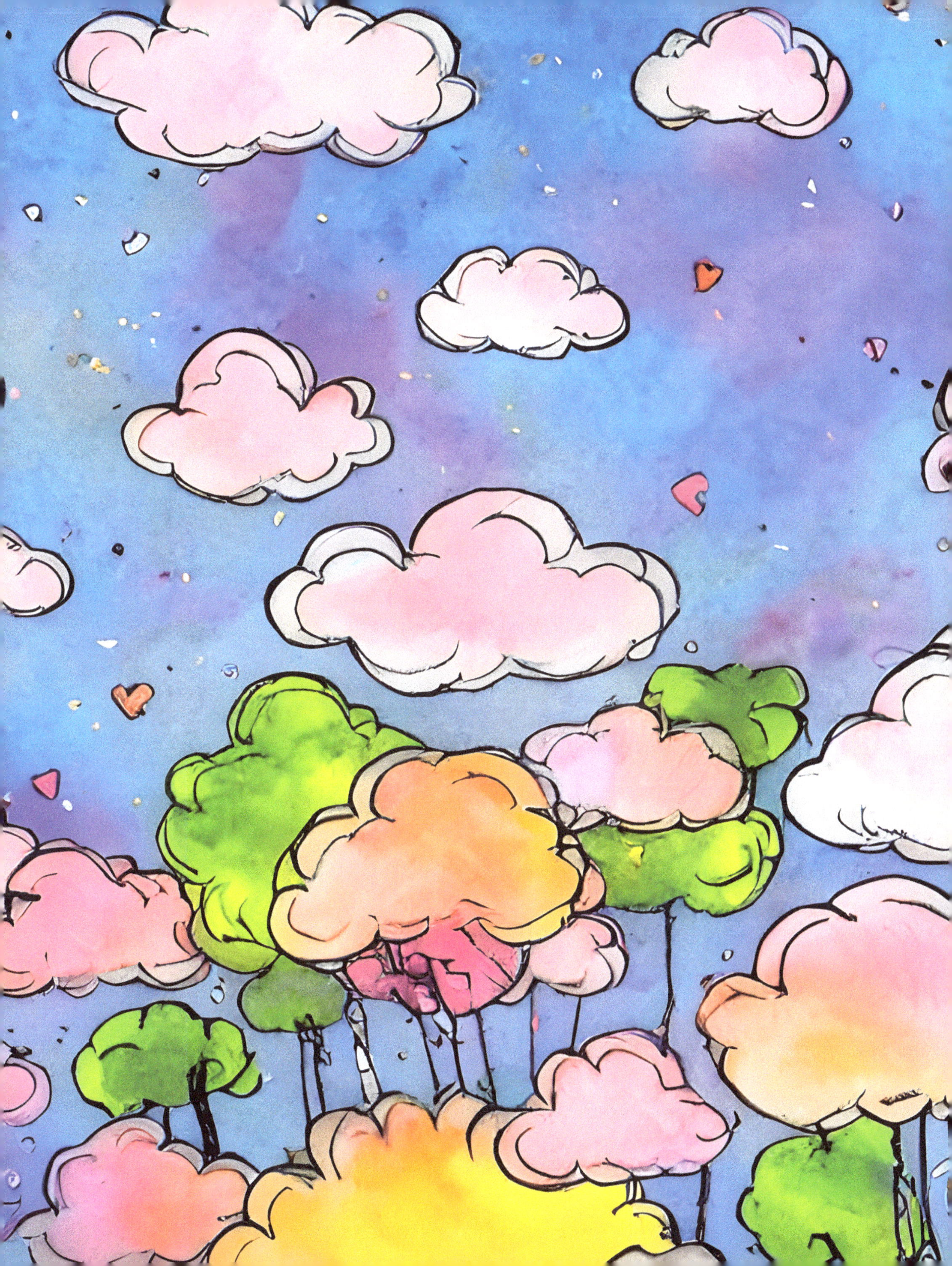

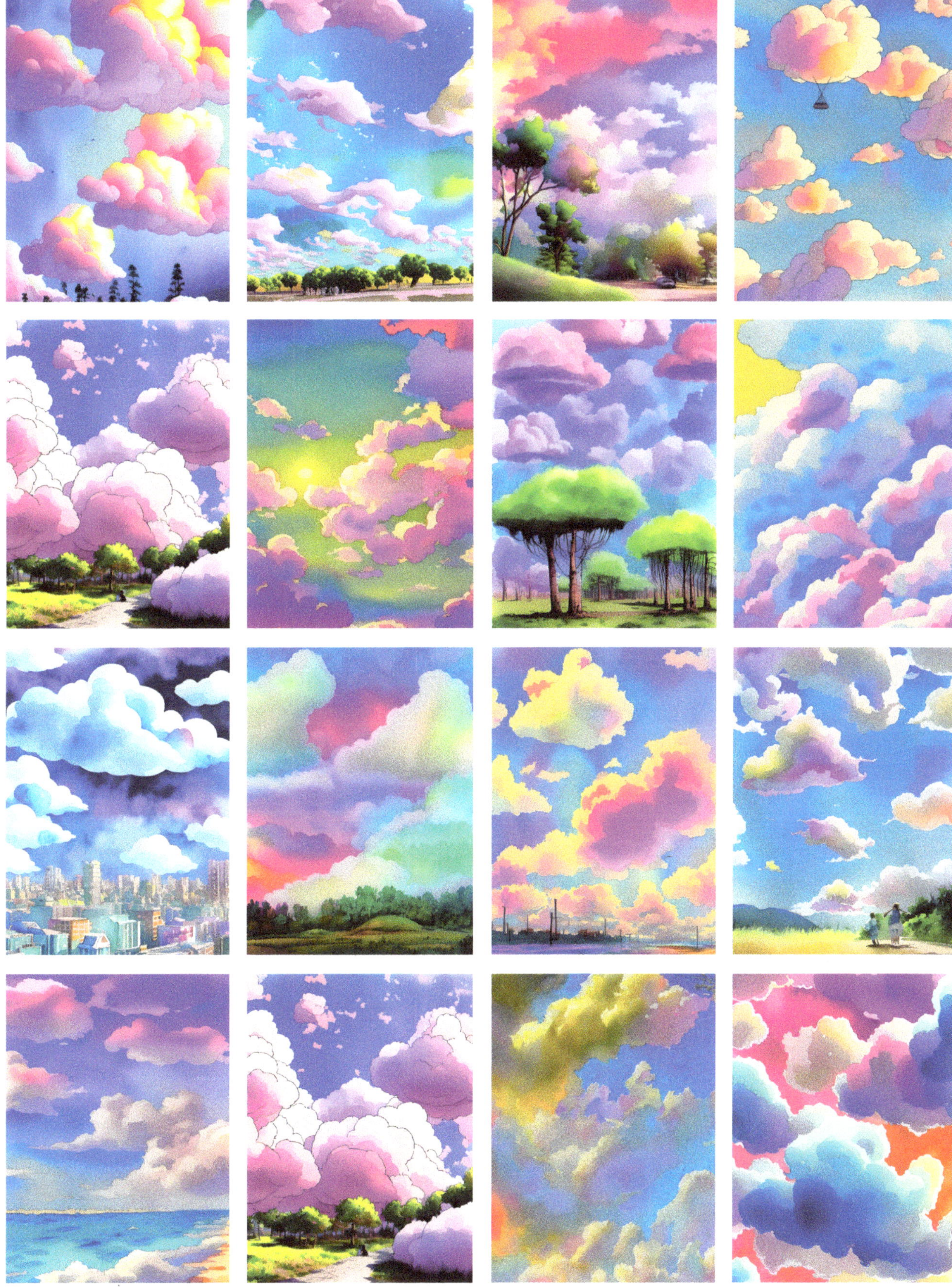

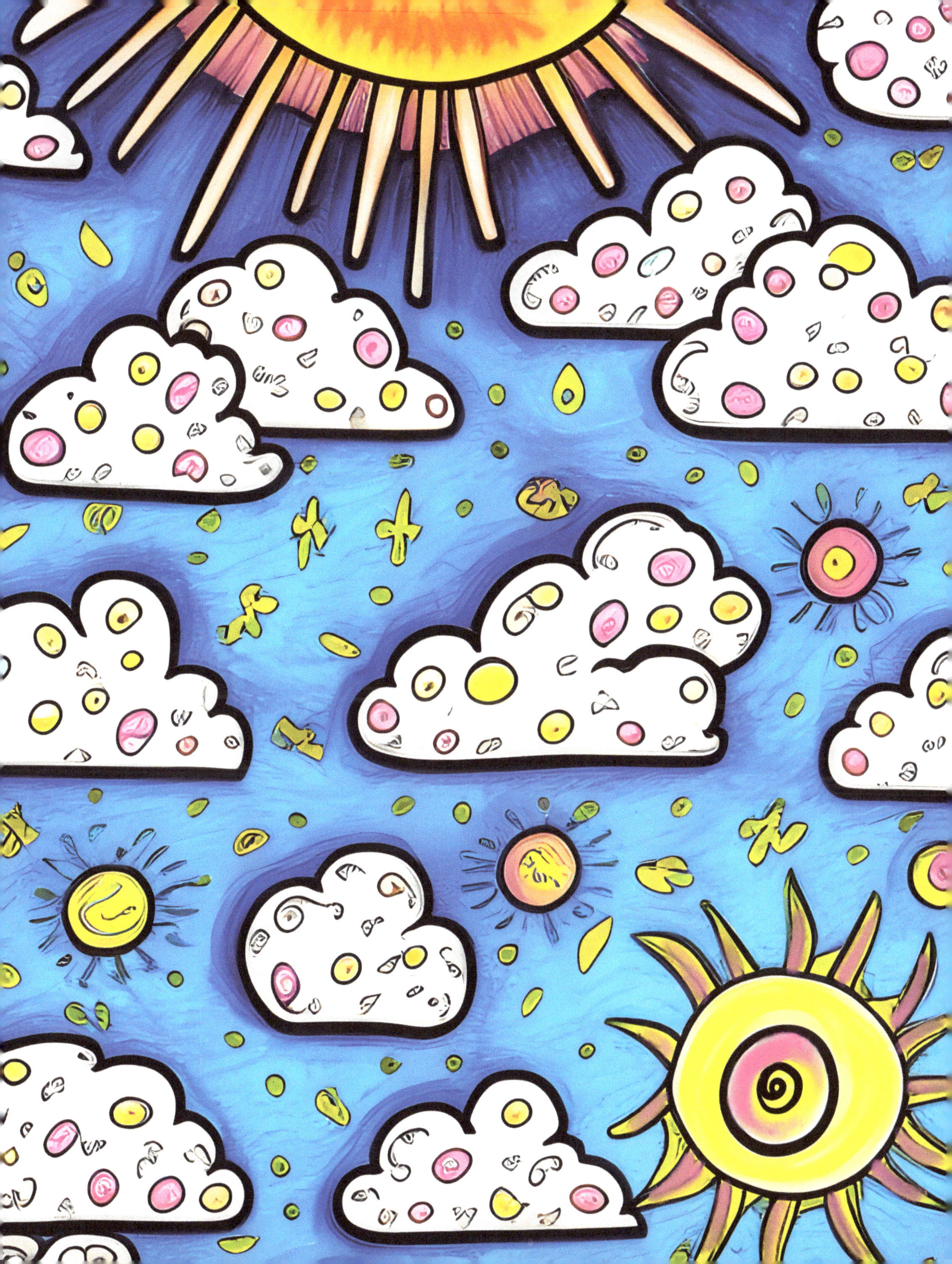

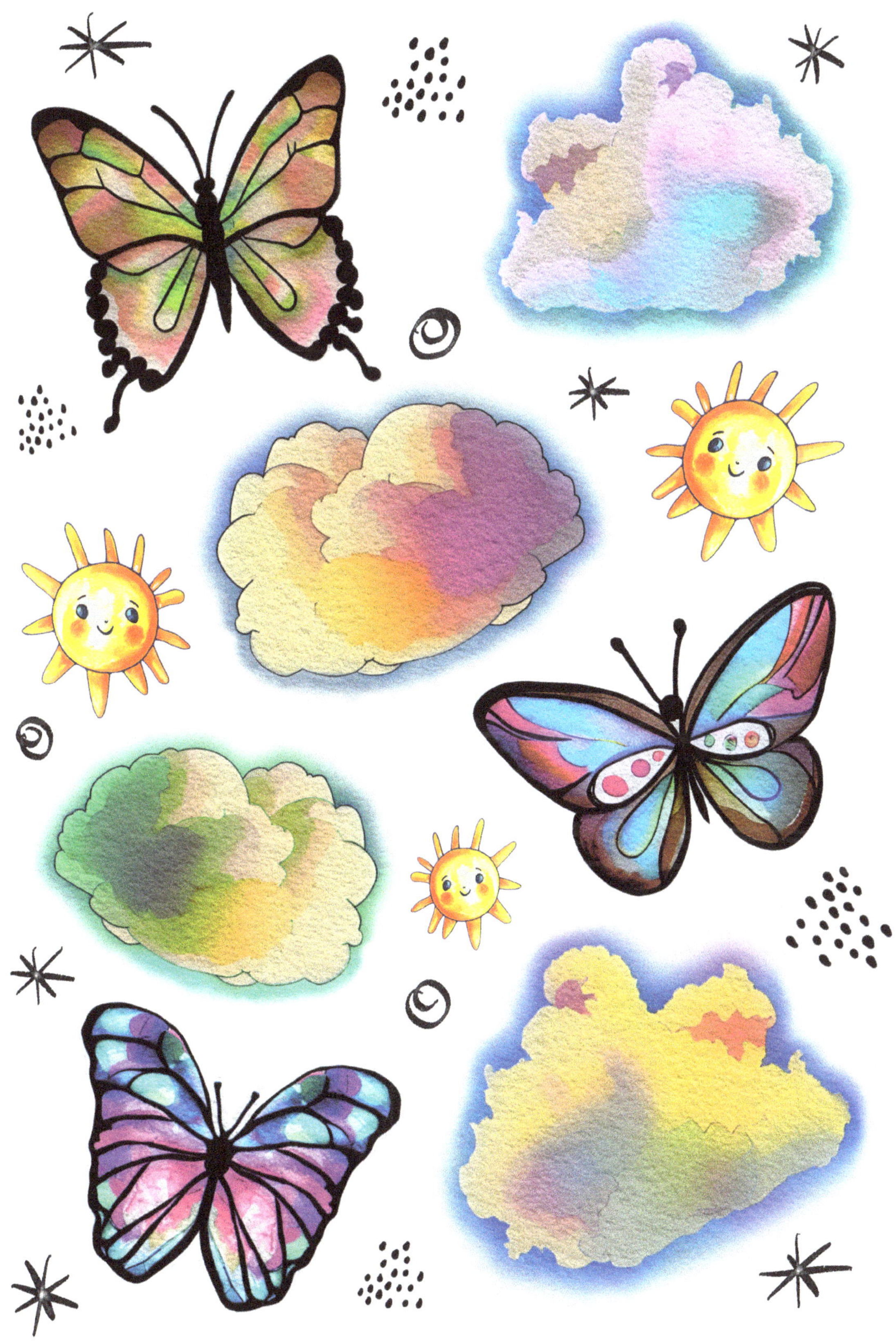

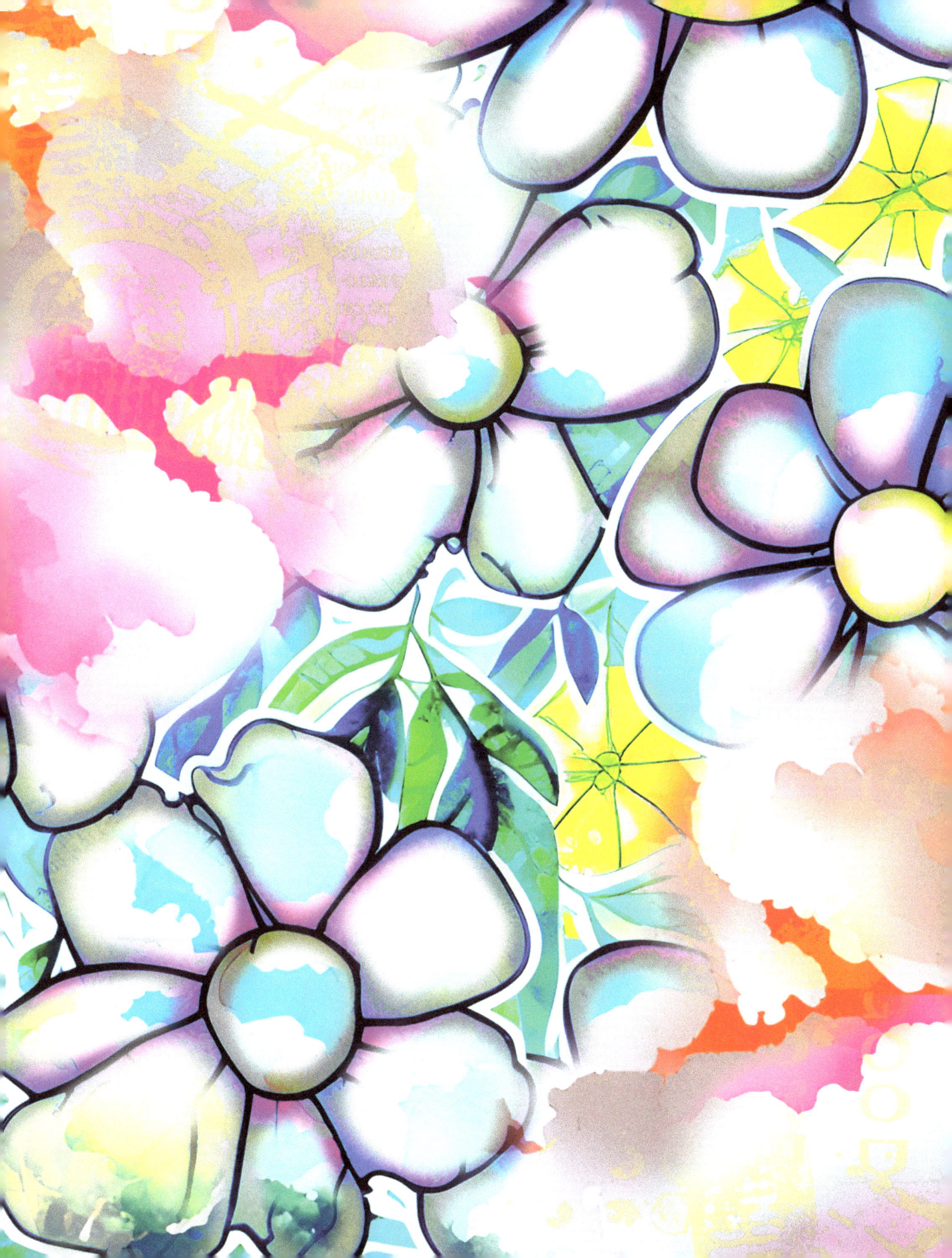

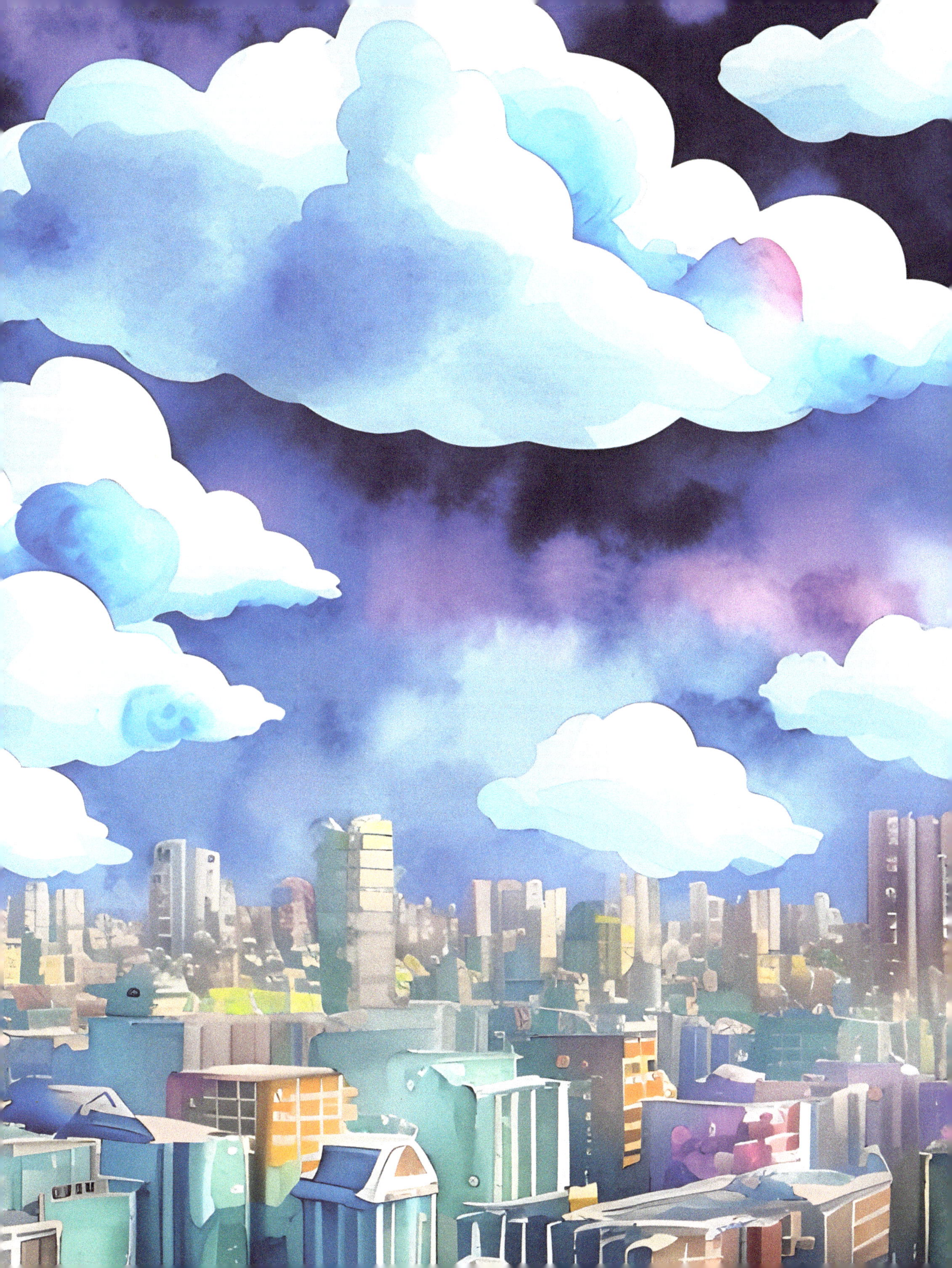

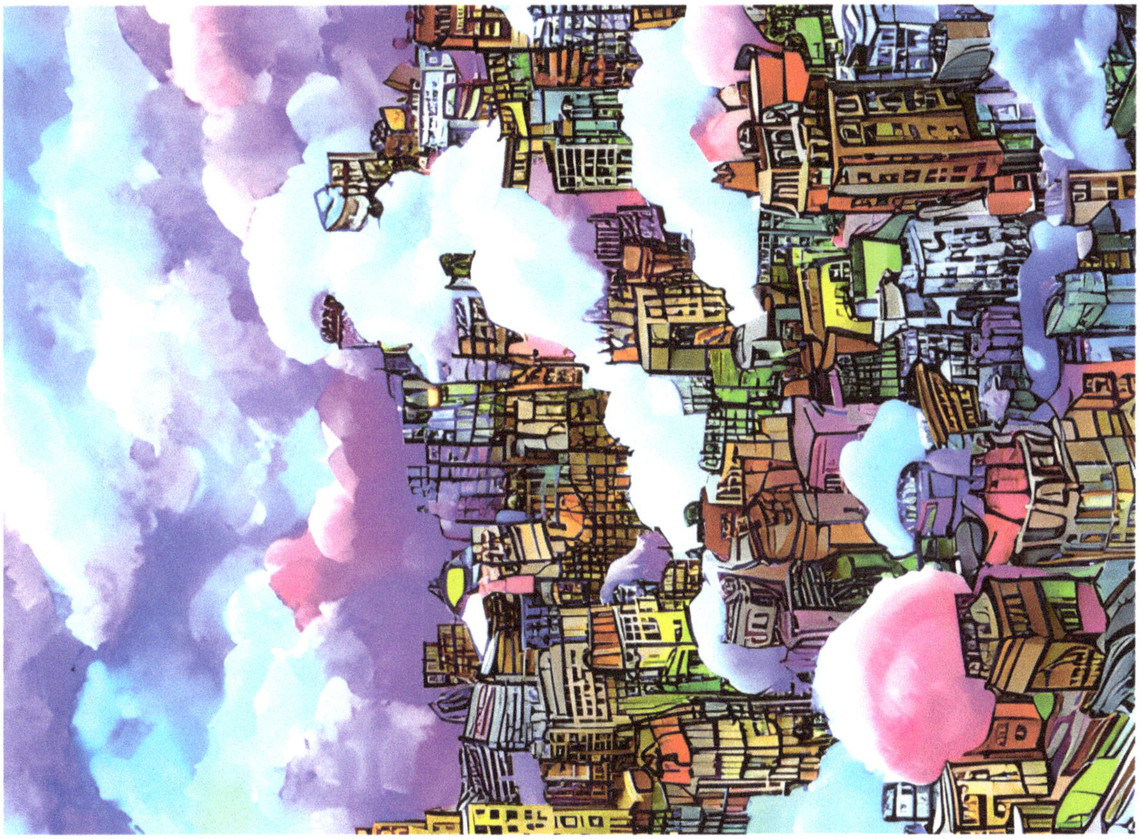

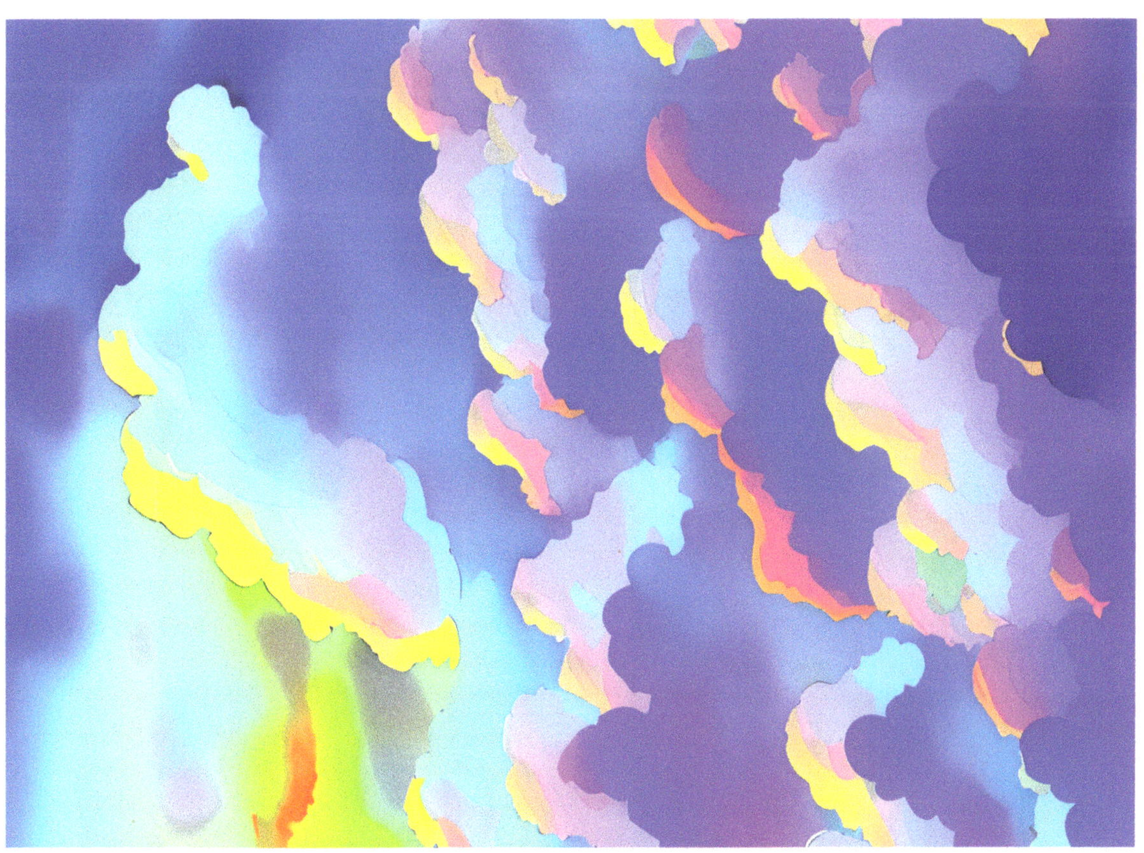

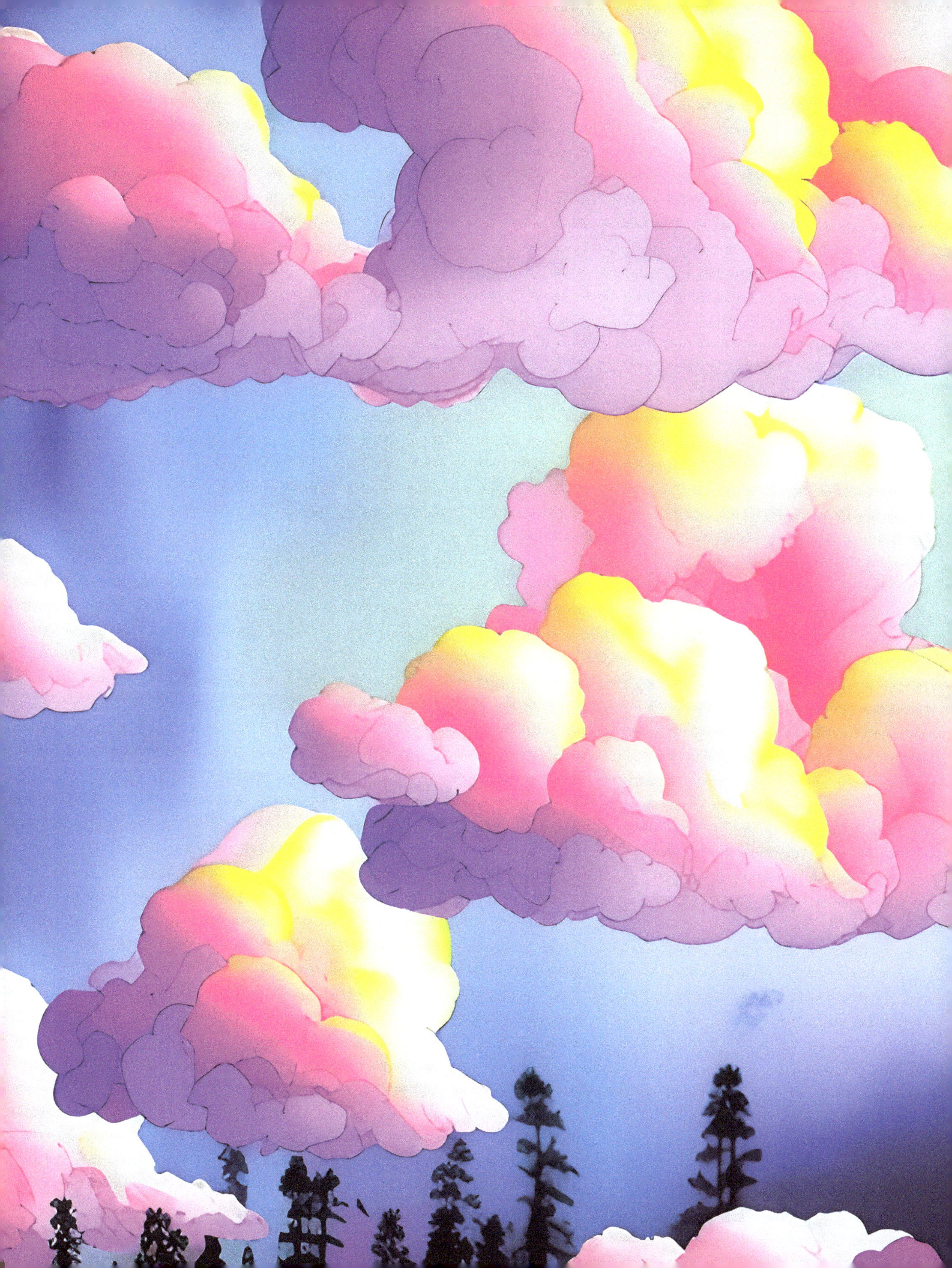

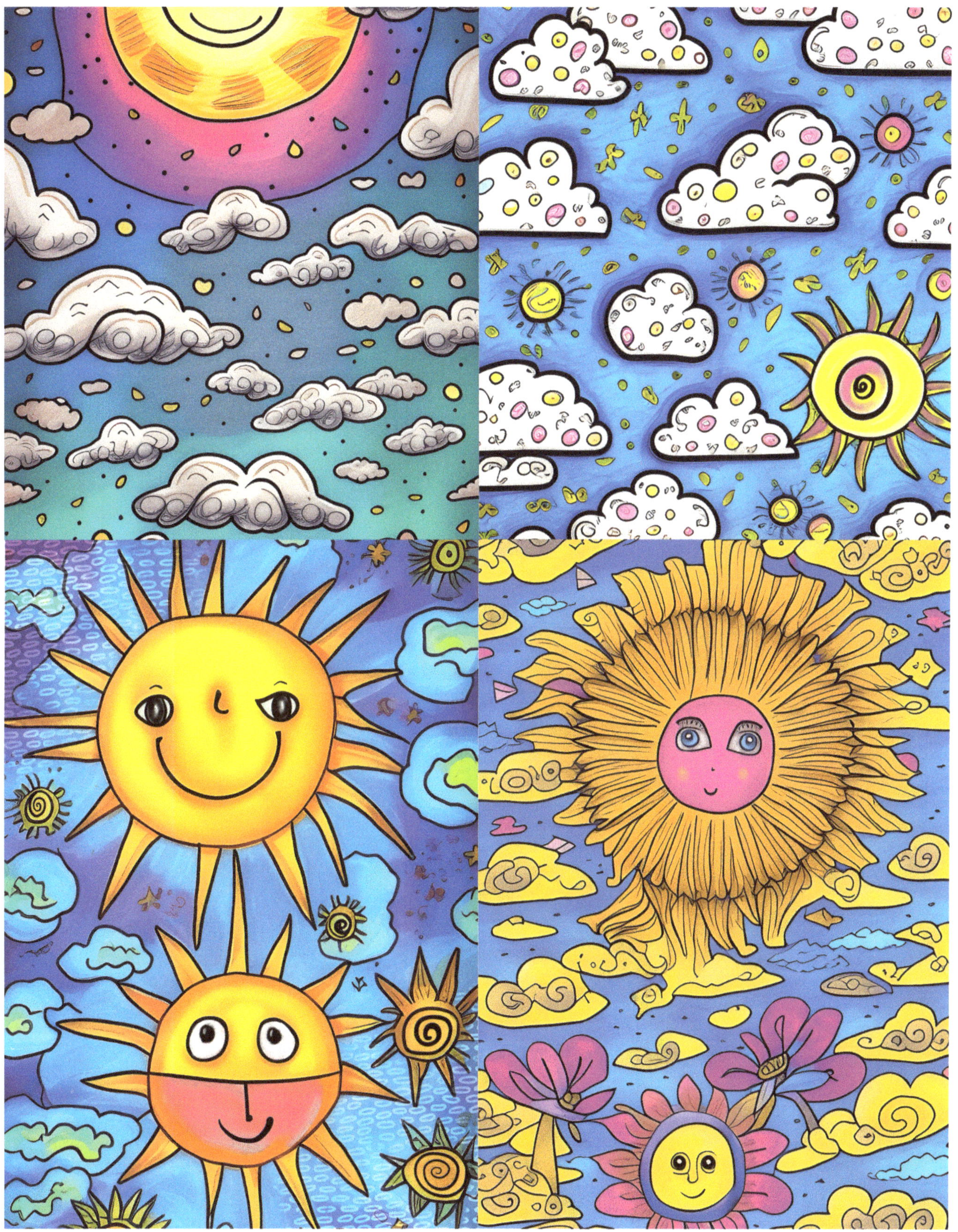